Praise for *The End Is the Beginning*

"Matthew Ian Fleming brings to his study of the book of Revelation his vivid personal memory, his alertness to popular culture, seriousness about the text, and a winsome imaginative sense of humor. The outcome of the work of his many gifts is an invitation to rescue the book of Revelation from the mistaken use made of it by fundamentalist literalists with their infallibility, inerrancy, and theology of fear. In the place of such distortion, he offers a reading of the book of Revelation through an engagement with its imagery and cadences. Fleming's rendering of the book will be much appreciated by those who receive the Bible and particularly the book of Revelation as the voicing of a world under God's gracious, relentless goodness. As Fleming reads it, that gracious, relentless goodness will, soon or late, prevail."

—**Walter Brueggemann**, William Marcellus McPheeters
Professor Emeritus of Old Testament at Columbia
Theological Seminary, and author of many
books, including *Prophetic Imagination*

"*The End Is the Beginning* is a generous companion to the book of Revelation, filled with personal and cultural connections that help us find new ways into this book and the wild ways it is baked into our lives. Matthew writes like he talks, making the dynamic and conceptual more accessible for the rest of us. His wonder is an undercurrent, pulling the reader into trusted company while we are reclaimed by good news and love that lights the sky."

—**Meta Herrick Carlson**, author of the Ordinary
Blessings series and *Speak It Plain*

"Through one of the most unexpected journeys, Matthew Ian Fleming leads us to discover a God who is present and 'making all things new.' I remember reading Revelation as a young person, almost secretly because it felt strange and mysterious. Wh
most about Fleming's work here i
reading the Bible. Part commentar

T0204906

interpretation, the book defies genre and helps us practice a relationship with the Living Word through engaging Revelation. As I see it modeled by Fleming, this means sharing our story with the Living Word, which is active and dynamic, and compels our imagination toward a beautiful world that we are called to bear witness to and usher in the here-and-now."

—**Mihee Kim-Kort**, author of *Outside the Lines* and co-pastor of First Presbyterian Church, Annapolis

"If you have ever looked out at the world and wondered if it was the end times, this book is for you. Rigorous and accessible, Matthew Ian Fleming guides us through the scariest book in the Bible, inviting us from fear back to love, where God's vision of a new world is revealed. As sage, storyteller, and scholar, Fleming's beautiful words teach, heal, invite, and inspire. The end is, in fact, the beginning."

—**Ellie Roscher**, author of *The Embodied Path*, *Play Like a Girl*, and *How Coffee Saved My Life*, and coauthor of *12 Tiny Things*

"Rev. Fleming grew up among Christians who understood Revelation as a blueprint for the end times, where the righteous are saved and the unrighteous are damned. Even as he left the Christianity of his youth for mainline Protestant communities that almost never talk about the end times, Fleming continues to be captured by this difficult-to-understand final book of the Bible. Here Fleming invites readers into Revelation by beginning with the ending, the promise that God is building a new heaven and a new earth, a place beyond all suffering and sorrow. Weaving his own story and stories of our current context together with stories from Revelation, Fleming illustrates how knowing the ending shapes all that comes before it, especially in terms of taking on the beasts, the monsters, and the dragons that try to thwart God's promised vision to which we all ultimately belong."

—**Deanna A. Thompson**, author of *Hoping for More* and *Glimpsing Resurrection*

The End Is the Beginning

THE
END
IS
THE
BEGINNING

Revelation, Hope, and the
Love That Lit the Stars

MATTHEW IAN FLEMING

BROADLEAF BOOKS
MINNEAPOLIS

Library of Congress Cataloging-in-Publication Data

Names: Fleming, Matthew Ian, author.
Title: The end is the beginning: Revelation, hope, and the love that lit the stars / Matthew Ian Fleming.
Description: Minneapolis: Broadleaf Books, [2024] | Includes bibliographical references.
Identifiers: LCCN 2023058888 (print) | LCCN 2023058889 (ebook) | ISBN 9781506497044 (print) | ISBN 9781506497051 (ebook)
Subjects: LCSH: Bible. Revelation—Criticism, interpretation, etc.
Classification: LCC BS2825.52.F533 2024 (print) | LCC BS2825.52 (ebook) | DDC 228/.06—dc23/eng/20240226
LC record available at https://lccn.loc.gov/2023058888
LC ebook record available at https://lccn.loc.gov/2023058889

Cover design: Brynne Worley

Print ISBN: 978-1-5064-9704-4
eBook ISBN: 978-1-5064-9705-1

For Hannah, who turns noise into music,
even the rhythmic patter of my keystrokes.

Contents

Introduction

I woke up early on the West Coast to our phone ringing. It was my grandfather. Curly quaffs of white hair hedged either side of a bald head sunburnt from working in the church yard, where he served as custodian. He would pay me fifty cents (don't I feel old now!) for every toilet I cleaned at the church, then take me to McDonald's for plain cheeseburgers and French fries, ketchup being far too spicy for a man born and raised on a pork farm in Kansas.

"The Pentagon was bombed. They're saying terrorists."

If you lived through this particular world-wrenching event, you of course know exactly where you were, exactly who was around, perhaps what you were eating or wearing. Memories seared into our brains, binding neurons together in unpredictable and formative ways that we recall with a snap. Some true. Some not. Some in between.

The man I called Papa, my grandfather, was a pillar in our church community. Before he retired as a lineman for Pacific Gas & Electric, he was on the board of elders, the men (yep, all men) who led the spiritual life of the church along with the pastor. He went to Promise Keepers rallies, listened to Christian radio (I can still hear the jingle between songs, "Positive, encouraging, more music, K-Love!") and later the angrier Rush Limbaugh and Fox News. An often tender and warm man to me and my cousin, he was also the first one to share with me a book called *Left Behind*.

I read through some of it, but I was far too busy with video games and riding my bike to slow down with a book about Jesus coming back. Oddly enough, I can't remember a pastor preaching sermons about end-times. I can remember plenty of hell and brimstone and anger with fists on the pulpit, but I don't recall words from Revelation or specific moments when a youth leader taught us about the rapture. Rather, it was in the air we breathed, in the culture we consumed. The *Left Behind* books were all on the bottom shelf of that small church library that I helped clean. The topic came up around the card table with my grandparents' friends from church. They were stories told late at night on a youth retreat. They were questions puzzled over at summer camp. And they were fiery altar calls in sweaty tents of Christian music festivals.

"Such and such preacher says that these are signs of the end-times."

"When the rapture comes, we'll all be whisked away."

"Do you know what will happen to all those who are left behind? Make sure you're not one of them."

These questions and more were swirling on that September morning in 2001. Are these the end times? Is Jesus coming back? Did the rapture just happen? Am I left behind? Am I going to hell? I remember my youth director—theologically trained with a great spirit of grace and hospitality, but who couldn't be called a pastor because indeed she is a woman—offered to open the church for prayer and conversation to some of us precocious high school students. Of course I went, sat on the cushioned chairs, sang the praise songs of the day, and listened for a word of comfort. I longed for an anchor of certainty, a promise that everything would be alright, a blessed assurance that God held me close. But it didn't come.

I remember staying late, sulking up to the front of our small church building, and asking sheepishly, "Do you think this is the end of the world?" It wasn't the first time I'd wondered about it. Because I was taught that the Scriptures help us interpret the world around us, there must have been an explanation from the Bible for the awful things I was seeing on the news. My youth director was patient with my questions but kept tying neat bows around them, bows that seemed to unravel immediately.

"Trust in the Lord's plan."

This event had broken through any semblance of my understanding that God had a plan for the world in front of me. There are events that shatter our expectation, that break through the realm of possibility and force us to reckon with what my twelfth-grade English teacher called "cursed questions." More than gut-wrenching, these events take on a cultural significance and become truly world-wrenching. I was cursed by the questions of rapture, end-times, a war between the forces of good and evil. I didn't know it at the time, but soon Evangelical leaders would prey upon those enigmatic themes with Islamophobic curses of their own. They would stir an imagination presumably from Revelation to propagate hatred toward Muslim people, codified in so-called patriotic laws of surveillance and discrimination.

But the more I read Revelation, the more I find that these leaders abuse the text, picking and choosing verses and conjuring ideas entirely their own to support whatever policy they are pitching. Long after sitting in those cushioned chairs in the small-town Evangelical church, I found myself teaching Revelation to an entirely different set of people. The Lutherans that I later taught had their own questions for Revelation. Most didn't read its verses with the same baggage. Their curiosity was formed by a lack of attention to the book at the end of the Bible, by a lack of exposure in church or Sunday school. So I got cozy with commentaries, snuggling up to some of the strangest corners of Scripture. Curiosity always my sharpest tool, I studied and I followed my questions and I found myself teaching a book that eventually had something to teach me.

In challenging myself to find glorious visions of promise and fierce words of indictment in this strange book at the end of everything, I found a new beginning of sorts, meeting a God who isn't electing between sheep and goats on judgment day but rather holding a community in loving embrace through a world-wrenching time here on earth. This God isn't damning creation and whisking the saved to a new heaven in the sky but rather preserving the possibility of creation with a love that lit the stars. I met a God who flings gates wide open. I met a God who battles forces of oppression and domination in upside-down apocalyptic acts of love, not fear.

If you'll join me, it's exactly this God that I'd like to introduce you to in the next chapters.

WHEN THE TOAST IS BURNED

It was a hot summer day, and fifteen of us were packed into a hot Econoline van, laughter echoing from every row of the standard-church-youth-group mode of transportation. We were on our way to an enormous Christian music festival. If you didn't grow up in Evangelical culture at the turn of the century (my daughters love it when I speak old-timey like that), these were about as rowdy as you can imagine. Unlike the Warped Tour that my "unchurched" friends attended, this festival had no booze, no dope, no nudity, but equal parts weird culture.

Need an example? One year three of us spent countless hours creating suits made of duct tape, which we wore while skanking to the horn section of the lively Christian ska band Five Iron Frenzy at the Air1 stage.[1] Another year, we made clothing from bubble wrap—highly impractical for a sixteen-year-old, running around outside in a northern California summer. Two letters: B.O.

This summer excursion was the highlight of our year as a church youth group. We would camp in the dusty hills overlooking

---

1 I write as an in-betweener. I grew up in a Christian culture that I don't belong to anymore (as has on occasion been made abundantly clear to me). And I serve a Christian culture (Mainline Christian, Lutheran) where very few people in our church have experienced the culture I was so formed by. I'll use these footnotes to offer some in-between. Sometimes I'll go a little deeper for those of you who were raised in various fundamentalisms. Sometimes I'll define some terms for those who might be curious about a world you've never been part of.

Monterrey Bay, then ride buses to hear all of the bands of the early 2000s play at the height of their national cultural influence, fueled by high fives and endless optimism.

But on the three-hour drive to this high holy day of Evangelical subculture, we were singing to our favorites. My addiction to Christian contemporary music (CCM for the in-crowd) began when the youth director at my parochial school offered to trade any secular CD or cassette for a Christian one.[2] It was his great joy to find a sound just like the one we swapped. A true rebel, all I had to trade was a hip-hop disc from Disneyland and Will Smith's *Big Willie Style*, which I'm fairly certain got me DC Talk's *Jesus Freak* and Newsboys' *Take Me to Your Leader* in return. Evangelical subculture blossomed in the early 2000s, creating industries of music, film, comic books, and novels that were separate from the secular industry. It articulated so-called "Christian values" that reacted to growth in women leadership in the workforce and liberation of queer people by harkening back to a *Leave It to Beaver* nostalgia for simpler times when people were more "moral" and "upstanding." I consumed this mechanism in school, in youth group, on the ever-present K-LOVE radio, in books shared among young men, and at Christian revivals and festivals like the one I attended that summer.

Our youth group had a rule whenever we were traveling. If we couldn't agree on tunes in the CD–cassette adaptor, our youth director would sometimes punish us by insisting on her favorite—Neil Diamond. Between eye rolls and Swedish fish, the disc changed tracks and the whole van erupted.

Thighs stuck to the vinyl seats of that fifteen-passenger Econoline, we shout-sang with hoarse voices and hands pushing at the upholstery on the ceiling. The Newsboys song toyed with the classic movie *The Breakfast Club*, remembering people who live without the

---

2 Parochial schools are private schools that are religious in nature. Math was math. Reading was reading, though we often read different books. But, in my experience, science was taught with a Bible bend (no evolution or Big Bang theories, for example). And lest I forget, we were graded on how well we memorized the Bible.

Lord, who have no hope, and pointing to various breakfast cereals that they will miss if they don't make it to heaven. With distortion guitar, peppy drumbeat, and the Australian accent of the lead singer, the chorus to the song reminded all of us that "they don't serve breakfast in hell."[3] While we laughed and smiled and danced, we were all haunted with the specter that at any given moment we could end up without Captain Crunch, living in hell instead of heaven. There is something about the strange charge of this song that really encapsulates the culture I grew up in. The fear of hell was real, as preachers fanned its flames in fiery sermons. And accountability groups encouraged constant vigilance for the prowling enemy who might drag us into temptation and damnation. But we *laughed* at it. We sang the choruses and snickered at the meaning, laughing and dancing until it hurt.

In a tent at the music festival, some of us would be swept up to the altar by a preacher who asked us if we knew where we would go when we die. Some of us would cycle in shame for the thoughts in our pubescent minds or the images we saw on the computer screen. Some of us would join accountability groups to make sure that we didn't stray into sin and jeopardize eternity in a lake of sulfur and fire. Some of us would stay up late reading leather-bound New International Versions, neon markers in hand, highlighting verses we didn't understand full of images of battles and monsters and demons whose punishment was far worse than missing a bowl of sugar for breakfast.

Underneath the sparkle of the synthesizer and the innocence of the tune was a message of fear and dread. "Work out your salvation in fear and trembling." "The wages of sin is death." That kid you know who didn't know Jesus who just died in a car accident. The uncle who lives with his same-sex partner of decades. The Catholic family down the street. The Muslim siblings in chemistry class. The girl with two moms who goes to the Unitarian church across town.

---

3 Newsboys, "Breakfast," *Take Me to Your Leader*, 1996.

They're all heading to eternal damnation. We knew that much. But who knows? I might be heading there too.

MISFIT SOCKS AND BIBLE BRUISES

My youngest daughter has a thing about socks that don't fit right. The little seam at the tip needs to be set right on top of her toes, not crinkled up at the corner or bunched off to the side or twisted at an angle. I can tell the moment she gets the sock on that it just doesn't work. She'll rip it off right away and toss it aside, needing an entirely different pair. My experience of growing beyond a faith that I inherited felt a lot like socks that didn't fit.

For a while I just stopped wearing socks. Who needs them anyway? I was happy in bare feet, though there were some places where they wouldn't let me in. Encountering the earth under my soles taught me much about seeing things from a different perspective. I listened to other people talk about their religious practice with curiosity rather than conviction. I wondered how science might actually answer questions that the Scriptures couldn't. I encountered friends who were coming out of the closet and dreamed we were beloved rather than abominable.

Eventually I met Jesus again, but he looked and sounded a lot different from the fists pounding on the pulpit growing up. I started to read about the tables that Jesus sat at, the people he dined with, the kind of company he kept. I started to understand that Jesus completely enraged the religious insiders. The people who would resist his preaching and teaching the most were the ones that the system worked best for, not the people living on the margins. Reading Revelation from a fresh perspective helped me untangle some of the strange knots of faith that I grew up with. Even more, it helped me tease out other parts of the Bible and grow toward a more hopeful vision of belonging.

So, to finish my sock metaphor, I started picking up the threads, buying some new ones, getting a new bit of elastic, unceremoniously stealing a scrap or two from a friend, and eventually wearing them more often than not. And now? Well, I'm getting used to the way the seam settles across the wrinkles of my toes. It isn't comfortable, but it will always be there. My faith is an inheritance that has been passed down to me, that helped someone before me even when it left me itchy—itchy and bruised.

One of the things that didn't fit well in this time was the Bible. For many people raised in mainline Protestant or Roman Catholic traditions, the Bible may not have been something that you interacted with regularly. The Bible was perhaps a family heirloom on the coffee table that Grandma told you never to touch. Or it was that book that the priest (or pastor) hauled out into the middle of church with all the reverence and pomp that comes with it. I didn't grow up with this understanding of Scripture.

For me, and perhaps for you if you were raised in a more Evangelical world, the Bible was a constant companion. It was the rule by which we were judged. It was a manual for morality. It was a script to be rehearsed and memorized over a lifetime. As my faith evolved and I began to question many of the traditions I was raised with, the memory verses sometimes stung like fresh cuts or ached like purple bruises. Stories like mine are not unique. Spend a bit of time on TikTok and find countless tales—heart-wrenching, humorous, discerning, hopeful, fiery, explosive, meditative, eager. I write from the other side of a process that many Christians (and post-Christians) are calling *deconstruction*.

I'll share some of my story in the pages ahead as a means to open up conversation to a whole world of people who are fleeing regimes and theologies that have bruised and buried. I will also share stories of people that have taught me about their journey with deconstruction, their witness to this strange book that keeps calling out, and the way they see God's love persisting in places we least expect it. This book is an invitation of sorts. As you read my story and the stories of the friends I have gathered, I invite you to take time telling your own story of faith, wondering how Revelation, the scariest book in the Bible, might have intersected with your life. I hope that you find surprising grace, delightful promise, and an insistent conviction that God is opening gates of welcome to a new beginning of creation, rather than damning souls to eternal torment. I hope bruises left by fear in your story receive balm of perspective and context. Most of all, I hope you can follow the thread through Revelation to find a new beginning in reading Scripture, listening for a voice that sang creation into existence with love.

THE SCARIEST BOOK IN THE BIBLE

My friend Shawna grew up in a Lutheran congregation in Arizona. Every year her little church would receive an intern from the seminary—a doe-eyed young person who was a bit too eager to help the teenagers learn about faith. Every intern wanted to teach from the Gospel of Mark. She assumed it was because they had just taken the class and so were confident they could provide the correct interpretation. But the teenagers didn't want to hear the same book every year, so they revolted time and again: "Teach us from Revelation!" Every intern would laugh awkwardly and move back to the Gospel of Mark, except for one. He issued a challenge that if they came back on Monday nights with their parents, they could all study Revelation together. He called their bluff but also took seriously the hunches they had about a book that seemed so strange. The whole class showed up Monday night, with their parents.

If the Bible is the family heirloom on Grandma's coffee table for many mainline Christians, Revelation is the section that fell out a generation ago and nobody has missed it. In my experience, Episcopalian, Lutheran, Presbyterian, and Methodist preachers rarely use Revelation. It infrequently occurs in the Revised Common Lectionary and is almost never the focus of preaching or Bible study.[4] Children rarely see Revelation's provocative images in storybook

---

4 The Revised Common Lectionary is a list of texts that is shared among a variety of Protestant Christian denominations. It uses a three-year cycle to explore the three synoptic gospels (Matthew, Mark, Luke) and sprinkles John throughout. Revelation shows up exactly eight times (across three years of Sunday readings) in this list of readings but is even more rarely preached upon.

Bibles, and few people will open its pages in a Sunday school, confirmation, or youth group session. Revelation has been neglected by many mainline Protestants, while Evangelical circles often issue troubling and even dangerous Predictions from its verses. My experience, however, is that even people who haven't cracked the spine of their Bible at home are curious about Revelation. It is filled with intriguing descriptions, curious contexts, pyrotechnic battle sequences, and ultimately, promise of God's sustaining love that lit the stars.

For many Evangelical Christians, the Bible is a manual for morality, and Revelation is what happens if you "fall into sin," as my accountability groups used to say. Even more, it's a prediction of how the end of the world will come about. For some on the fringe, Revelation is even a calculation of when the end of the world will arrive. For people who grew up in neither of these communities, Revelation appears all over the place in popular culture. It's the butt of a joke for a militant atheist, source material in a comic book, and a reference for every post-apocalyptic story told on page or stage or screen.

Revelation has been used to wage wars through battle cries that still sing from many of our hymnals with lines like, "Mine eyes have seen the glory of the coming of the Lord, he has trampled out the vintage where the grapes of wrath are stored." Revelation haunts the dreams of zealous adolescent dreamers and late-night apocalyptic salesmen. It's rippling under the surface of contemporary suspicion of fringy religiosity with phrases like "drinking the Kool-Aid" that ironically recollect the mass murder perpetrated by apocalyptic cultist Jim Jones. Revelation is studied as high literature in college classrooms through the poetry of Milton's *Paradise Lost*, Dante's *Inferno*, or Yeats's "The Second Coming." Revelation is source material for Q-Anon conspiracy theorists and punch lines in cartoons like *South Park* or *The Simpsons*. Revelation can offer nightmare fuel if you don't have enough to keep you up at night. Our task, together, is to not stay mired in the scary, strange, and sometimes gory images of Revelation, but to listen for the whisper of God who is sustaining all that was and is and will forever be and is calling to us from the pages of this ancient book.

A KEY

Before we get into the deepest corners of Revelation, I want to introduce you to a type of key. No, it's not a secret code that will unlock the mysteries of the universe. It's not a way to decode the strange numbers in Revelation and make a prediction to win the stock market. It's a key to clinging to an understanding of God that might be challenged in the verses that we will read together in Revelation.

In an entirely different part of the Bible we find Psalm 139, a song I first read closely when I was a canoe guide in northern Wisconsin. Sitting on the shore of the largest freshwater inland sea in the world, I could recite from memory the few verses that we shared at the end of a week-long excursion with teenagers.

> "Where can I go from your Spirit?
>   Where can I flee from your presence?
> If I go up to the heavens, you are there;
>   if I make my bed in the depths, you are there.
> If I rise on the wings of the dawn,
>   if I settle on the far side of the sea,
> even there your hand will guide me,
>   your right hand will hold me fast."[5]

Revelation will take us to the height of heaven and to the depths of despair. We will encounter beautiful, ecstatic imagery, and we will see horrific destruction. So my invitation is to use these verses as a guide throughout this voyage into the strange corners of Revelation. Oddly enough, in the very same psalm, in a few verses where most have likely never read, we hear this call:

> "If only you, God, would slay the wicked!
>   Away from me, you who are bloodthirsty!"

---

5 Psalm 139:7-10, NIV

There is a remarkable dance in the hymnal at the center of the Bible. A back-and-forth ballet between words of promise and callous confessions. Revelation paints colorful canvases of God's love and tender care for all of creation. At the same time, it gives voice, poetry, and special-effects-worthy battle sequences to a longing for real power to change here on earth. We will spend time looking closely at both, but it is important to keep the consistent image of God's love at the core. Like Psalm 139 reads, we can't go anywhere without God's presence. Not the heights of heaven or the depths of *sheol*, the pit, the land of the dead, the farthest place from the heavens. God is leading and guiding us wherever we find ourselves, even in the seemingly strangest pages of Scripture.

ECONOLINE REVELATION

In the back row of an entirely different fifteen-passenger Econoline, I closed my eyes and took a deep breath. Nineteen years old and exhausted, I was escorting three early-teen girls from the trail. Slightly defeated and ending our five-day excursion down a crystal-clear river full of sturgeon, I was trying to diffuse a skirmish and get the kids home safely. These girls swam and laughed and sang. They also cried and fought and swore and pushed against every attempt to build belonging. Their adult leader, a fierce social worker who served three years in the Peace Corps, was a saint. But they got to all of us.

On this four-night canoe trip, we settled into a ritual every evening. Exhausted by coaxing smoky trail water into dehydrated and defiant youngsters, the three adults would strategize for the next day, tending one another, listening for the stories that slowly started to crack open. We slowed our pace, adapting to the immediate needs of this small group of young women. We wouldn't push them to paddle to the landing at the end of our journey. Making it only a quarter or half mile down the river each day stretched ample space to sleep in. We cooked breakfast before they woke up, let them float, swim, and *sing* down the river. The kind of community we were introducing was foreign to these girls. The social worker who traveled with us described various attachment disorders, represented in diagnoses within the group. We felt the impact of their symptomatic withdrawal, trained (often in infancy) with parents who could not support their wellbeing, and later formed through our flawed foster care system. Anytime someone appears safe, kind, and welcoming, every fiber of their bodies resists the feeling of settling into the embrace of belonging. Reacting against a feeling of love, some of these young women would fight back, pushing away with every tool at their disposal from *colorful* language to fists and feet.

The back seat entirely to myself, I called camp from the driver's cell phone to let them know we were coming back early and that I would only arrive with these three of the ten girls. The others would stay at the landing with the social worker and my co-guide, still shaken, to process the fist fight that erupted and to keep them safe. After hanging up with the camp director, I closed my eyes for who knows how long. I flashed back to twenty minutes earlier, when these three girls were pushing the others into the river, shouting obscenities on the landing, spitting, swearing, punching, kicking, and screaming. "If you need to punch someone, you can punch me," I'd said. One fist knocked the wind out of me and hurt more than my youthful masculinity wanted to admit. The social worker and my co-guide separated the girls and locked them in a bathroom, just as the van pulled up. Adrenaline pumped jet fuel through my veins, and I was lifting canoes onto the trailer, hoisting Duluth packs into the van, as the girls giggled in the front bench of the Econoline.

I was angry. I was tired. My nearly eternal optimism plummeted to the bottom of the river to be swallowed by sturgeon. I crawled to the very back seat of the van to separate myself as far as possible from these three. But something otherworldly happened. I can't explain it. I can only say what I heard: *singing*.

"Sometimes in our lives,
we all have pain.
We all have sorrow."

One of the girls looked through the rear-view mirror right into my eyes, singing at full volume, *Lean on me.*

I don't think these girls knew a lick of Revelation. We didn't talk Bible or God or anything spiritual. But in the back of that Econoline, I think I caught a glimpse of the vision that John spins in this strange book at the end of the Bible.

A vision of a God who wipes every tear from our eyes, who dwells among us, and who feeds the world with love and peace.

A vision of churches who build belonging, affirm belovedness, and stand up for movements that matter.

A vision of faith that means as much in the last breaths of life as the fearful gasps of world-wrenching events and humdrum beats of daily living.

A vision of worship that beckons a better world and forms humanity in stillness, song, and celebration.

A vision of victory that banishes beasts that prowl in the marketplace and devour the livelihoods of people across the planet.

A vision of paradise that rewilds the parking lots of empire's might and provides food and healing for the nations.

As I looked into the eyes of these young women, I saw the pain. I saw the sorrow. Singular stories that cry with the pain of all that is. But they weren't crying at all. They were smiling, singing with pride and invitation, almost daring me away from despair, to dive into a promise that I barely believed for myself. A promise of a God who would go to the end of the world and back to welcome me into the arms of mercy and grace and love. A promise of a God who would battle the armies of destruction and despair and injustice and oppression to sustain a community. A promise of a God who would damn the systems that fracture the souls of young people like these in order to sit slowly, beckoning belonging with patient sips of water that rehydrates dry bones with the sweet spring of creation itself.

Like these two stories of Econoline vans, Revelation is a series of cycles with beautiful, ecstatic worship and dreadful, terrifying visions of death. We will confront monsters and demons and Satan himself as a dragon devouring the mother of God. We will count numbers and read symbols and engage a deeply political vision that uproots the powers of empire and calls forth a kingdom without end. It will take work. It will take energy. I won't blame you one bit for putting this book down and walking away from Revelation. I've wanted to send these socks to the landfill more than once.

But Revelation persists in my imagination, and it puts its elbows on the table of our current moment. Wars are raging, pandemics are spinning into divisive acrimony, the climate cries out for a change, and the daily scroll looks more like a post-apocalyptic comic book than a news update. Reformers and preachers have minimized Revelation in commentaries and lectionaries, studies and classrooms. Revelation dreams of a God who is in the midst of the heartache of our times, wiping away our tears and watering the fertile soil for new growth.

I need these images of God in my life as much as the first followers of Jesus needed Revelation's fiery verse. Beasts prowl our contemporary world in wars and famine and plagues and conspiracies and the never-ending onslaught of an economic model that ships profit to the top and squeezes more sweat equity from everyone else. Revelation provides a framework for resisting the powers of this world that seem insurmountable. It shakes me out of apathy through the subversive power of ritual, song, and verse, replacing my weary world with unrestrained acts of imagination. The God I met in the strange verses of Revelation interrupts my daily programming with a dream that shatters every commercial break and disrupts the incessant echo chambers of doom scrolling. Through all of Revelation's dreamy worship sequences, pyrotechnic battle scenes, many-headed beasts, and confounding mathematics, God whispers a simple promise where the end really is the beginning: "Behold, I am making all things new."

If you'll join me, it's exactly this God that I'd like to introduce you to in the pages to come.

1

What Revelation Is Not

A BOOK WITH BAGGAGE

My friend Natalia leads a Bible study for people who have been wounded by church, who are asking questions and coming to conclusions that their faith can't keep up with. They study an entire book of the Bible in one hour—a wild challenge. At the beginning of every Bible study, she asks the group to name what they have inherited or heard about that particular corner of Scripture. The responses range from quiet ignorance to twinkly-eyed curiosity to dogged stories of religious trauma. The Bible carries a lot of baggage for many of us. It has been passed down (often largely distinct from the text on the page) by narratives in church schools, youth groups, family gatherings, and summer camps. As this curious small group reads each chapter and verse, they are often delighted, surprised, and confounded by what they find. They uncover new contours of the narrative, nuance to the characters, or context they had never gathered before. I've become sort of addicted to that "Aha!" feeling in myself and when I can see it in others.

Perhaps you've heard that Revelation is full of superstition and hooey. Perhaps you've heard that it contains the secrets to the mysteries of the universe. Perhaps leaders have used these verses to tell you where you are going when you die. Perhaps you recall late-night

Bible studies in student unions debating pre-millennialism. Perhaps you've never ventured into this corner of Scripture. Perhaps you haven't studied Scripture much at all but remain curious about the book that so many obsess over.

To be honest, Revelation has baggage, maybe more than any other book in the Bible. And yet it is a book that very few people have *actually* read. There are certainly churches who focus quite a bit on end-times—one example is the Seventh Day Adventist church. I grew up adjacent to many Seventh Day Adventist[1] family members. My stepmom was raised in Thailand, where her parents served as missionaries, attended college at an Adventist university, and traveled the world teaching in Adventist schools. When I was in eighth grade, we visited her parents in Vietnam, where their religious convictions informed their development work—supporting orphanages and schools for the blind, building hospitals, and witnessing to Jesus where it fit. I am inspired by their service, dedication, and willingness to follow the challenges of Jesus quite literally. Their faith always seemed to follow directly in Jesus's footsteps, expecting to meet Jesus where he promised to be: among the widow, the orphan, the refugee.

It was only later that I realized how much of Adventist theology is informed by the immediate expectation that Jesus is returning again. When she was young, my stepmom attended Revelation seminars, a curriculum designed to teach about the second coming, their specific interpretation of this strange book, and how the ongoing discipline of practicing Adventist Christian spirituality would prepare them for the coming of Jesus. Discussing this over dinner decades later,

---

1 If you are unfamiliar with Seventh Day Adventists, they are likely known best for the simple fact that they worship on Saturdays rather than Sundays, following (strict or loose, depending on the family in my experience) adherence to sabbath principles expounded by their founder, a twentieth-century prophet named Ellen White. While this book isn't about the various forms of fundamentalism, I like to share bits and pieces of this world for those of you who have not spent any time in it. Evangelicalism or fundamentalism is not monolithic. It varies dramatically across the United States and the world.

it was like I bumped into another example of how the last book of the Bible had shaped my upbringing. I hope this book helps each of us find ways that we inadvertently bump into Revelation even if we've never read it before. We will be bold enough to speak back to narratives that are less than helpful and listen carefully for the promises of God that are lurking right under the fear that many of us have inherited.

I won't be teaching you a Revelation seminar. We will not be reading Revelation verse by verse (though I'm not sure my stepmom did in her seminars either). Rather, I'll be sharing stories, connections, analogues, moments in history, pieces of art, and popular culture to apply the strange images and visions from this book to our ordinary lives. Slowly, story by story, we'll see together how the way we read Revelation influences all sorts of decisions from foreign policy to environmentalism, questions of our origins, and imaginations of our endings. While few of us may have yet cracked the spine of Revelation, its imagination is everywhere we look, whether we are in church every Sunday or never darken the door of a local congregation. I hope that this book might be a companion to Revelation. As I share bits of my story and the way that Revelation has intersected and interacted with me, I hope that you might be emboldened to wonder the same about your story and dare to read these strange pages with curiosity and courage. If we can confront together some of the misinterpretations of Revelation, I'll be pointing us toward the promise that resides in this strange text. We need to dig through the baggage a little bit, look carefully at the contents, wonder how it has informed our stories of faith and our interpretation of God's work in the world. But eventually, I'm going to invite you to put it away, zip it up in heavy-duty luggage cases, so that we can find together a new way to read Revelation. I'll be showing the way toward the God that is proclaimed on these pages. It will take pulling up some weeds, digging deeper into the contextual soil, and imagining our own context with curiosity and courage. But in the end, I think we'll find a new beginning to our relationship with Scripture and with the love that lit the stars.

STORIES FROM ANOTHER WORLD

My eldest daughter loves to ask me about the times when I grew up. From the backseat, when I always have NPR playing, I hear, "Daddy, turn off the news. I have a question." Before bed, to delay the inevitable and explore something unknown, "Daddy, tell me a story about when you were a little boy." At nine now she teases me, "Did you take tests in school with pencils and paper? And there were no iPads? And you rode to town in a covered wagon?" She has a sense that the world *before* was vastly different than the world *now*. And she's right. These conversations remind me how quickly the world has spun into something unrecognizable.

My family has lived in the same small town in northern California for three generations. I can remember asking the same questions my daughter is asking me, but I vividly recall the bluster coming from my father: "This. town." The congestion and development of the community belied a shift in values that escaped anything he could recognize. He wanted out. What once were orchards and dairies had turned into vineyard upon vineyard upon winery upon tourist upon Michelin star upon Tesla upon endless wealth on display. In my dad's lifetime, this rural, agricultural town of dairy farmers and walnut groves became a playground for tech money and bougie bachelorette parties. Stories now drip from the vines, not of catching crayfish in Dry Creek but of terroir and possibility in every sip.

When my daughter asks me to tell her stories of my childhood, I attempt to share images of what it was like. Mavis Beacon teaching typing on the Christian school computer lab, crunching words as they fall from the top of the screen. Riding bikes in endless summer, quarters jingling in my pockets to buy grape soda and Reese's at Ranch Market. Exploring an abandoned military base on the edge of town with flashlights, jumping fences and wandering in ruins from just a generation gone by.

It's a practice of storytelling that my grandmother taught me, and my father after her. They would share a world entirely inaccessible to me, but I can still recall the most compelling tales: Uncle Bill's epic adventures in the sawmill. Little Grandma playing the grand piano in her parlor. Swimming in cold aqueducts in the Central Valley.

When we open the pages of Revelation, we are opening a world that has even fewer cultural anchors, tilting its appearance into categories of strange and apparently inaccessible. Rather than four generations, we are hundreds of generations removed from the people who first witnessed this vision rending the heavens. In just a few dozen years, the world I grew up in looks nothing like the world my daughters inhabit. After so many generations, Revelation seems incredibly strange to us. The landmarks are gone, the references have shifted, and the stories have changed. We can't step into Revelation expecting to understand every shift and beat without a little context and imagination.

If you wrote down the five things you did before sitting down to read this book, very few of them would intersect with the world that Revelation speaks into. My list might provide an example for your own story:

1. I made a cup of coffee. (People wouldn't start drinking it for another fifteen hundred years.)
2. I turned on the lamp. (Light bulbs wouldn't be invented for nineteen hundred years.)
3. I sat down in my armchair. (Mass-market furniture again wouldn't be available for another forty-five generations.)
4. I opened my spiral-bound notebook and wrote a few phrases with a ball-point pen. (Many folks would not have been literate and would not have had access to expensive paper and writing implements.)
5. I flipped the switch on my e-reader to get lost in a novel written halfway around the world. (The world was starting to stretch, but local concerns reigned.)

I know this seems like common sense. Duh! But this is not common sense for those of us with various fundamentalist Bible bruises. Many of us were taught that God wrote the Bible with a really long pencil that stretches through time and space, bringing us in contact with eternal truths that speak the same to us as they did thousands of years ago. This is a very strange approach to a book (or rather a library of books) that is more than three thousand years old. It is a simple way to describe how we can read the Bible, but it evades the depth possible when comparing ancient context with contemporary realities. I'm not here to say that Revelation should stay stuck in the ancient world. Rather, by engaging in interpretation, wondering about its meaning, and learning about the context, we dip our toes into a river that stretches all the way back to the earliest followers of Jesus. We ask our own questions, ponder our own meanings, and listen along with the generations of Christian ancestors who have come before us.

I was taught in parochial school, sermons from the pulpit, massive revivals, and weekly youth group that the Bible is inerrant and infallible. The Bible contains no errors—no spelling mistakes, grammar errors, or historical inaccuracies. These two words (inerrant and infallible) are likely the biggest distinctions between different Christian communities in the U.S. context. For those who cling to these doctrines of Scripture, the Bible becomes a solid rock, the foundation of a system of beliefs that is built on a set of verses. The texts are carefully chosen, highlighting some and shuffling others off to the margins. Propping up all sorts of claims about the role of women in leadership, moral judgments on contemporary issues like capital punishment or same-sex marriage, these beliefs and verses are the fundamentals (where we get the word fundamentalist) on which Evangelicalism stands. But for those on the inside, it can feel like picking at that foundation might bring the whole house down. How can we trust that God loves us without certainty God wrote these words? How can we know we're going to heaven if there are inconsistencies in the Scriptures? How can we believe in God creating us and everything that exists if the Bible doesn't tell us how? Speaking from personal experience, chipping away at these doctrines often left me confused and scared. It led me to interrogate a worldview handed down by the people I loved and trusted the most. Even more, for many Evangelical people, belonging depends on adherence to these doctrines. Expressing doubt might mean losing friends. They might fear that you'll be a poor influence on their kids or break off platonic or romantic relationships. How you read the Bible influences what you think about politics and morality and values—or maybe it's the other way around?

Most Christians—whether Evangelical, mainline, Roman Catholic, or Orthodox—will have some understanding that Scripture is God's word for us. But how we understand that word and its relation to the whisper (or shout) of God's voice among us is vastly different. With words like "inerrant" and "infallible," it is as if God dictated the words to Paul or John or Moses, and they are speaking to us directly. Other Christians might say that the Bible is divinely *inspired*. It reflects the time and place of the author and is shaped by their faith and trust in God's guidance of their witness. By focusing on inerrancy or infallibility of Scripture, context is often sacrificed for a clearer understanding of God speaking directly to us from the pages of Scripture. One of the troubles with this approach is that it underplays the important work of interpretation.

Every reading of a verse or story or chapter or book of the Bible is an interpretation. The Bible has been translated from Greek or Hebrew or Aramaic to English, which itself is an act of interpretation. Some words cannot be translated well into a modern language with a single term. Others carry multiple meanings or vary in the surviving manuscripts from antiquity. Any reading of the Bible has been shared from a particular vantage point in history and society, perhaps from a white woman who grew up working class in Virginia in the 1970s—interpretation. It has been shared from a particular theological tradition or stream, perhaps from a United Methodist congregation that grew like wildfire when it started incorporating contemporary music and larger Evangelical culture—interpretation.

But inerrancy and infallibility are not the only way to read this text (or any text in the Bible). Instead, we might speak of Revelation as coming from the words of John, an imaginative writer with an ecstatic vision of God fighting hordes of very real centurions and chariots, defending a small sect of Jewish and gentile followers of a rabbi from Nazareth. We might begin to imagine how this vision brought hope to a community that was experiencing persecution, that was scattered in small home churches and was afraid of what their future would be. We might wonder how Revelation's vision applies to various religious groups experiencing persecution around the world—Uyghur Muslims in China or Christians in Palestine. Understanding the ancient context of the Bible doesn't distance it from us. Rather it brings us closer to the people who first heard its words so we might understand more clearly what the Spirit might be speaking to us today through its verses.

Inerrancy and infallibility actually *limit* readings of the text. By insisting on a so-called "literal" interpretation of the Bible, the religious teaching that formed me effectively penned the stories in. It sealed up the rough edges with copious amounts of Elmer's glue and crafted a neat and tidy interpretation of Scripture that results in sanitized doctrines. It turns God into someone who sits atop a throne, passing down eternal truths like a transparent slide on an overhead projector (a metaphor that my children will have no relation to!). By getting curious about the context, the poetry, the symbolism, and the metaphor, we can begin to play with the text a bit more, noticing that it is not quite as rigid as we once thought. We can wonder about the motivations of the authors of the Bible, the specific challenges that kept them up at night, the concerns of their communities, and their personal dilemmas. We can begin to see that God is moving in all the aspects of the stories of Scripture, through a variety of voices who complement and even at times compete with one another.

When we read Revelation, we are reading a vision, recorded or shaped or drafted or preached by a specific person living nearly two thousand years ago. The shapes of the hillsides, the glimmer of the Mediterranean Sea, the feeling in his body when imperial Roman soldiers marched through the streets. All of these images are likely inaccessible to us. Further, John writes in Greek. While it is not a dead language, contemporary Greek is very different from ancient Greek. Scholars with decades of training in ancient languages continue to debate nuances in language use, and many of the subtleties have been lost to time. Many of us might tune in to the apocalyptic intrigue of fiction like *The Last of Us, The Handmaid's Tale, The Matrix, Mad Max,* or *The Hunger Games,* but our vantage point is often shaped by being on the victor's side of history, rather than the ones being trampled by an occupying army or crushed by unjust economics. Contemporary people may find entertainment or distraction in the reversal of politics and economics rather than a vision of hope through turning the tables of might and victory upside down. In linking such a misreading of a text like Revelation to an eternal doctrine of biblical inerrancy, we both dodge the political indictment of the text and tuck it neatly into a dogma supposedly handed directly from God. Instead, I invite us to get curious about both the historical context and its contemporary applications, listening for the voice of God that is still speaking from the margins, surprising any with ears to hear, unveiling good news that isn't static dogma but a cosmic call that shakes us out of apathetic accumulation and consumption with revolutionary practices of song and story, prayer and worship. If we are too busy shoring up doctrines of inerrancy, we will miss the subversive song of Revelation that stretches from the first breaths of creation to contemporary cries from our city streets.

All this is to say, I have a hard enough time imagining the small town I grew up in the way my dad experienced it. My daughter can't imagine a world without the internet and mobile devices. When we approach Revelation, it is very difficult to say, "God says this" with utter confidence that we know what that means, to distill an eternal truth out of a messy and hasty vision.[2] Our challenge, rather, is to get curious about the text, start to pull at its fabric, and find the threads that stretch across Scripture, ancient context, and into our daily lives. We will explore together the streams that Revelation

---

2 If all of this is brand new to you, I encourage you to perhaps pause a little bit. This is a huge shift in how we read and approach and understand the meaning of Scripture. There are many approachable books that will use much easier texts than Revelation to help understand this way of reading the Bible. A few of my favorites include Rachel Held Evans's *Inspired*, Peter Enns's *How to Read the Bible,* and Rob Bell's *What Is the Bible?.*

offers us, the images of Jesus, and the persistent promises of a God who is sustaining all that was, all that is, and all that will be. In the mystery, wrestling, and pondering, I believe God is still speaking in and through these strange visions. But to get at the heart of its message, we'll have to do some weeding first.

LEARNING THROUGH ELIMINATION

On the side of our house is a patch of ground once covered in landscape rock. Year after year, soil settled on top of the weed cloth set beneath the stones, giving ample room for weeds, shrubs, bushes, and even volunteer trees to completely overtake this little pocket of paradise. One summer, we decided to tackle this project, slowly uprooting the weeds, clearing away the soil, moving the rocks out, putting new weed cloth down, and eventually creating a little garden with a pond that we enjoy with morning coffee or as the summer sun sets behind the trees. My back is sore just remembering how much time it took to prepare this small section of our yard. In many ways, we are *weeding* our interpretation of Revelation, pulling out images that aren't helpful any longer, removing shrubs of stories that obscure the original vision, so that we might see clearly what John saw and wrote. Once we can sit in the clearing, we can start to wonder together what this vision might be speaking into our own world.

When we open the Bible, we are opening a library of books that were written with vastly different concerns from our own. We can't step into the shoes of the ancients, just like my daughter can't know the feeling of a sharpened number-two pencil filling in the blue bubbles of a Scantron booklet. Historical criticism attempts to reconstruct these rooms, shed light on the puzzles, explore the ancient ruins. But inevitably it cannot open all of the doors of understanding in these ancient texts with the same colors and images that the writers imagined when they were penned. The process of interpretation leaves us with some work on our end, to contend with the visions recorded on the page, ponder how they might have looked to the people who first heard them aloud, and listen for the voice of the Spirit who enables us to understand Revelation's call in our lives, in our time, and in our world.

Sometimes it's easy to write off scholars as those writing in ivory towers who get too far in the weeds for us to take anything from it. And sometimes they do. The training of biblical scholars is incredibly rigorous, studying ancient languages, archeology, and the long legacy of biblical interpretation that stretches back to the earliest memories of the church. But all (fine, most) of the biblical scholars I've come to know do their work as an act of faithful imagination, helping us understand how God is still breathing through these texts written so long ago. They bring their concerns, their hopes, and their dreams to each text they interpret. At their best, scholars wrestle with the text and point us toward an interpretation that is faithful and applicable. I'm humbled and honored to introduce you to a variety of Biblical scholars throughout the pages that follow, who have shaped my imagination of Revelation. By bringing ancient context into conversation with our contemporary concerns, they help all of us hear the text more clearly and wonder together how God might be speaking into this moment.

As we open one of the strangest books of the Bible, we need to confront some of the things we've been told about this book. We need to look misconceptions squarely in the eye, and for many of them, we need to say no. Revelation is not saying that. We need to pull up those weeds so that we can see the flora creeping up through the cracks.

Many Christians are having a big conversation about the word "deconstruction" right now. Folks raised in various fundamentalisms are sifting through the layers of meaning they have inherited, pulling at the threads of a faith that was passed down, editing the interpretations, and questioning the assumptions. Some walk away from faith entirely, finding the system too painful to endure. Others are rewriting the scripts and rewiring their practices to reform something that fits their experience of good news.

I write this book as someone who has been through both of these responses. I grew up drenched in Evangelical subculture. To paint the picture for those of you who didn't grow up in this culture, I'm talking about Christian music festivals, megachurch revivals, Promise Keepers rallies, *I Kissed Dating Goodbye*, Relient K, Michael W. Smith, accountability groups, and straight-edge skateboarding. When I picked up *Harry Potter* for the first time, my grandmother was sure to warn me of the occult. When I brought home a CD with a parent-advisory label, I lost privileges (and of course the CD never made it out of the plastic wrap).

When I started to leave the faith I was raised in, venturing out in search of something different, it felt incredibly disorienting. I was the kid in youth group who knew all the answers to the questions, whose hand would shoot up with pride about any Bible story. But when my questions didn't have simple or easy answers, the systems started to fall apart. At first my old faith felt like an itchy sweater that never quite fit right. But soon enough fresh blood emerged, followed by scabs, scars, and bruises. It felt like many of the bruises came from the Bible, from texts I had memorized, or lessons I'd been taught. Deconstruction has been the process of working through these texts and these bruises, learning more about them, wrestling with some of them, and walking away from others.

All the while, Revelation keeps haunting me, keeps beckoning me back. It keeps rearing its ugly head in politics and the world, in overheard conversations at the coffee shop and on the airplane. Our spiritual ancestors in the Christian tradition have wrestled with its place in the canon. The Reformers, who influenced much of my theological training, were fairly unimpressed by the book. Martin Luther didn't find much value in the book. In the preface of Revelation that he translated into German he remarked that "Christ is neither taught nor known in it."[3] John Calvin, another famous reformer, was completely silent on Revelation. He wrote commentaries on every

---

3 "Preface to the Revelation of St. John," *Luther's Works*, vol. 35, trans. Charles M. Jacobs and E. Theodore Bachman (Philadelphia: Fortress, 1960), 399.

book in the New Testament except Revelation.[4] And yet, Revelation remains in our Bibles, calling out for each generation to interpret and reinterpret. Even though preachers rarely choose to preach from it, the liturgies of many of our churches draw from Revelation's poetry for hymns and confessions, liturgical music across the centuries. Luther may have been skeptical that Revelation can help point people toward Christ, but he drew from its images regularly in his campaign against the papacy. With the advent of the printing press, woodcuts on pamphlets displayed the imaginative description of the beasts and Satan in political cartoons against the Pope and Luther's prosecutors. Further, some of Luther's most hate-filled speech against Muslims in Europe likened their advances to demons in Revelation. And if we don't contend with it? If we leave it alone, or leave it to the noisiest interpreters . . . well, let's just say that's not such a good idea.

WHAT IS AT STAKE?

As I was finishing the last few chapters of this book, I overheard a conversation in a coffee shop. Two white men in their sixties were openly discussing a conspiracy about a ring of coastal elites trafficking children, supported by the media and the military-industrial complex. About ten minutes in, one of the men started to unfold Scripture-like passages from the latest Q-Anon post.

Perhaps you heard about Q-Anon[5] from a relative on Facebook. Perhaps you listened to a podcast or read an article. This twisted

---

4 Craig Koester, *Revelation and the End of All Things* (Grand Rapids: Wm. B. Eerdmans, 2001), 12.

5 "QAnon is a decentralized, far-right political movement rooted in a baseless conspiracy theory that the world is controlled by a cabal of Satan-worshipping pedophiles known as the 'Deep State,' which can only be stopped by former President Trump, and that these individuals will be brought to justice during a violent day of reckoning known as 'the Storm.' QAnon-linked beliefs have inspired violent acts and have eroded trust in democratic institutions and the electoral process." Anti-Defamation League, https://www.adl.org/resources/blog/qanon-resurgent-twitter

and (do I need to say it?) completely unfounded conspiracy theory revolves around a set of proclamations shared on social media message boards like 4Chan. In each so-called Q-drop, an anonymous author, named Q, publishes obscure messages full of insider language, open-ended questions, wild accusations, doctored photographs and memes, predictions, and visions. By piecing together these messages, followers around the world have built an entire mythology of conspiracy. If you've never heard of it, gird your loins for a moment because it gets wild. Q-Anon spins a story that all commerce, politics, and power are controlled by a global cabal of Satan-worshipping pedophiles who are well-known billionaires, politicians, and celebrities. The only person who can save the world from this terror is the forty-fifth president of the United States, who rides a white horse to save the world from certain destruction. But what does this have to do with the Bible? Or Christians? Or Revelation? Everything.

Even if you haven't read a lick of this scary book at the end of the Bible, I'm sure you can imagine what I mean when I say that that the kinds of images used in Q-drops sound oddly like verses from Scripture. They don't sound like Jesus sharing a story or healing the sick. They don't sound like the hymns and prayers of the Psalms. They draw from the stranger corners of Scripture, the apocalyptic texts (cue eerie music). Q, who remains an anonymous figure to this day, frequently references Scripture, including the more fantastical verses found in Revelation, Ezekiel, and Daniel. If you grew up with apocalyptic sermons, references to the second coming from the pulpit, or the occasional dated prediction of the end of the world, it will come as no surprise that Q-Anon conspiracy theories run rampant throughout Evangelical churches in the United States and across the globe.[6]

---

6 "QAnon is, in effect, one part Frank Peretti spiritual warfare, one part Left Behind series apocalypticism, and one part Elders of Zion antisemitic conspiracy theory, packaged together in a tantalizing, self-involving variation on Celebrity Apprentice reality television and social media." Jason Springs, "Zombie Nationalism: Canon, Conspiracy, and White Evangelical Apocalypse," *Contending Modernities*, June 16, 2021.

Q-Anon is not an interpretation of Revelation like some of the other Evangelical predictions of the end of the world. But it absolutely relies on an imagination rooted in Revelation and in very specific interpretations of its contents. Q-Anon positions a faithful few who are battling against forces who threaten to devour their way of life, offering hidden pathways to resistance through encoded messages and memes. It centers white conservative Christians in a war for more than culture and arms defiance with rhetoric that sounds more like Scripture than a think piece or social media thread. These interpretations play on the worst sides of Evangelical subcultures—white nationalism, anti-Semitism, racism, xenophobia, and homophobia. And they thrive because of the careful cultivation of an embattled identity among Evangelicals, many of whom believe they are a remnant, living in a country that is going right to h-e-double-hockey-sticks.[7]

Our interpretation of Revelation matters. There is a concept in teaching called the null curriculum. What we say *nothing* about actually articulates *something*. Those who avoid Revelation in Sunday school or sermons communicate its lack of importance. For most mainline Protestants and Roman Catholics, Revelation is part of a null curriculum that has dangerous consequences. Proponents of Q-Anon stormed the Capitol of the United States to prevent Congress from certifying the 2020 election. They posted crosses on state capitol lawns and conspired to kidnap the sitting governor of Michigan. It is essential work to articulate what Revelation is not, because very few congregations are offering a vision of Revelation at all. By avoiding the weird book at the end of the Bible, we are actually fertilizing the soil for bloody brambles and noxious weeds. These dangerous interpretations quickly take root through social media and even breech the foundations of our democracy itself. Weeding the overrun parts

---

7 This may skip a few steps for those of you that remain in Evangelical cultures. But this attitude of defensiveness against the dominant culture is well-established in politics and pulpit. For more read: Kristin Kobes Du Mez. *Jesus and John Wayne: How White Evangelicals Corrupted a Faith and Fractured a Nation* (2020).

of our communal yard gives us space to sit in the ideas and hear the compelling witness that Revelation can speak into our time. In the clearing we can meet the God who opens gates of belonging and sustains all of creation with love that lit the stars. We can encounter the unique contribution of Revelation that is only found in this little corner of the Bible, giving it room to speak in our faith and getting curious about how it might shape our perspective and practice. But first, let's pull a few of the more common weeds in our common yard interpretation of Revelation. Revelation is not a code to be unlocked. And Revelation is not a manual for the end of the world.

REVELATION IS NOT A CODE TO BE UNLOCKED

I returned to my home church for a reason I can't recall. It is always strange entering a space that you have wandered so far from. The pastor took time before the sermon to address the most recent "prophet" who calculated the end of the world. If I recall, this particular preacher had miscalculated the first time and then revised his prediction when the original date came and went with no scent of brimstone. My hometown preacher that morning was calm and patient, using much of his sermon to encourage people not to be misled by fringe prognostications. The pastor knew that the people in the pews (actually chairs in this case) were concerned about the proclamation, that they might be influenced by this kind of prediction. I don't think I've ever heard such a notice in a mainline Protestant church. Protestant preachers might respond to contemporary events as a preface to a sermon—a shooting in the neighborhood, economic crisis, or debate in the local school board. But rarely are my colleagues addressing fringe interpreters of apocalyptic literature from the pulpit. It isn't in the water.

In our increasingly segmented echo chambers of social media, we are not experiencing the same world. We are not encountering the same crises. We are not looking at news and events in the same way. We're swimming in different waters. Q-Anon conspiracy theories can spread so quickly through Evangelical circles because they seem to clarify obscure passages from Scripture, tying events in the news to verses from the Bible. They play on interpretations of Revelation that pay closer attention to the doors that God shuts, the vengeance that is visited, and the people who are left behind, rather than the work that God does to sustain all of creation. If you can't understand why anyone in their right mind would follow some of these conspiracy theories, you're likely swimming in different water, consuming different media, living in a different echo chamber. If you, like me, were trained from a very early age to look to the Bible for answers to everything, it might not be all that surprising that someone is sharing strange predictions on the internet, tying together strange bits of news with odd descriptions of Daniel or Revelation.

We didn't have cable until I was in middle school, so I would watch it occasionally at friends' houses, sneaking the occasional *Simpsons* episode that wasn't allowed at home. When we (*finally*) got a basic plan, two of my favorite channels were Discovery and the History Channel. Some of the reality programming was just beginning with *Dirty Jobs* with Mike Rowe or the terrifying stories of crab fishing in Alaska. The History Channel brought to life the textbooks from school. At that young age, I wasn't aware of how much the channel twisted scholarship so that it might boost ratings. I remember seeing frequent series on the apocalypse. Titles such as *Countdown to Apocalypse*, *Revelation: The End of Days*, and *Doomsday: 10 Ways the World Will End* brought so-called experts who would decode strange passages in Scripture in order to understand when the world might come to an end. In the year 2000, the news emphasized the Y2K computer bug, and I recall hearing murmurings and conjecture that this fulfilled prophecy for the end of the world.[8]

---

8 I won't chronicle or really contend with the many predictions of the end of the world because they don't pass the sniff test for most of us. A couple of other books do: Bart Ehrman's *Armageddon: What the Bible Really Says About the End* and Barbara Rossing's *The Rapture Exposed: The Message of Hope in the Book of Revelation*.

There is nothing new about looking toward Revelation and finding strange sorts of predictions. In many ways the text lends itself to these kinds of readings. Like Q spinning cryptic drops on social media, taken out of context, the visions from Revelation can fuel an endless number of strange (and often dangerous) readings. This is part of the reason that many of the great theologians and thinkers of church history have discouraged people from reading it.

Two functions of the text enable these strange calculations. First, the imagery is incredibly fiery—bowls of pandemic, a dragon scraping a third of the stars from the sky, beasts coming from the sea, strange marks on people, and lakes of sulfur and fire to name a few. Ancient people likely would have understood most of the references Revelation makes, laughing at the caricatures and gasping at the reversals. But, thousands of generations now removed, these seemingly obscure images tend to fuel the folks who look to Revelation as a blueprint for the apocalypse. Second, there are all sorts of numbers that show up throughout the book of Revelation. Sevens and twelves, which might be expected by anyone who has read other sections of the Bible. But sixes too, and triple sixes (666), and even more baffling numbers. Why does the dragon scrape one third of the stars instead of half or a fifth or 7,897? Why does the woman flee the dragon into the wilderness for 1,260 days? Combining Revelation's penchant for strange numbers (which we will look at in-depth in the pages to come) and its strange visions almost invite odd predictions. And it has. For two examples from very different contexts, consider Rasputin and David Koresh.

I first heard of Rasputin from one of those late-night History Channel specials. The story felt like unearthing a puzzle because it had all the ingredients that were off-limits—a dose of mystical religiosity, a cup of political coziness, a sprinkle of history, a dash of the occult, and the entirely forbidden—oodles of sex. Christopher Lloyd voices Rasputin in the animated *Anastasia*, and, more recently, Rasputin appears on Netflix's *The Last Czars* which dramatizes the story of the fall of the Romanov dynasty in Russia. Rasputin was a traveling mystic and healer who cozied his way into the heart of St. Petersburg aristocracy near the end of the Russian Empire and the Romanov dynasty. In a time marked with spiritualism and curiosity of the occult, Rasputin performed what appeared to be miracles for the wife of the Czar of Russia and their son, gathered devoted followers, and perpetuated abusive sexual exploitation. The History Channel pointed to Rasputin's prophetic tasks, predicting events that would come, including his own death, the death of the Czars, and the upcoming revolution in Russia. Relying on entirely questionable "experts," the shows then used Rasputin's writing to pontificate on signs of the end of the world in recent memory. Rasputin's predictions became source material for *X-Files*–like accounts of ancient alien theories and apocalyptic predictions because of the vague nature of the texts he left behind. In the all-knowing tone of the enthusiastic narrator, it is easy to be convinced that we might find some hidden message or code lying in the reeds of these texts, fueling speculation and fear even today.

Rasputin's growth in influence and coziness to the royal family scattered rumors across Europe from aristocrats in St. Petersburg to soldiers on the front lines of World War I. Seeing Rasputin as a threat to the stability of the throne, a group of Russian elites conspired to murder him, leading his assassin to perpetuate even more myth in his memoir: "This devil who was dying of poison, who had a bullet in his heart, must have been raised from the dead by the powers of evil. There was something appalling and monstrous in his diabolical refusal to die."[9] Oddly enough, this recollection sounds surprisingly like the beast from Revelation: "One of its heads seemed to have received a death blow, but its fatal wound had been healed."[10] Shortly after Rasputin's death, the peasant class revolted against the aristocracy and the monarchy in the Russian Revolution. While the myth of Rasputin's death is certainly not the reality, descriptions at scriptural proportions reveal ways that this strange mystic haunted

---

9 Carolyn Harris, "The Murder of Rasputin, 100 Years Later," *The Smithsonian Magazine*, December 27, 2016, https://www.smithsonianmag.com/history/murder-rasputin-100-years-later-180961572/

10 Revelation 13:3

both the elite few and the rising revolutionaries: "To the emergent Bolsheviks, Rasputin represented the broader problems with czarism. In the aftermath of the Russian Revolution, Provisional Government leader Alexander Kerensky went so far as to say, 'Without Rasputin there would have been no Lenin.'"[11]

David Koresh did not woo the political elite or make his way into the social class. Part of a radical Seventh Day Adventist sect called the Branch Davidians, Koresh led a cult headquartered at the Mount Carmel Center outside Waco, Texas. In 1993 the Bureau of Alcohol, Tobacco, and Firearms and the FBI laid siege to the compound. After negotiations broke down, U.S. government officials attempted to take the site by force. Throughout the course of the fifty-one-day siege, four federal officials were killed, as were eighty-two members of the sect, twenty-eight of whom were children. Before the FBI launched a final incursion on the compound, Koresh was dictating an interpretation of the seven seals found in Revelation: "Then I saw in the right hand of the one seated on the throne a scroll written on the inside and on the back, sealed with seven seals, and I saw a mighty angel proclaiming with a loud voice, 'Who is worthy to open the scroll and break its seals?'"[12] Koresh believed he was the only one worthy to break the seals that would bring about the return of Christ.[13] He preached to all who would listen that he could unlock the code in Revelation, therefore ushering in the end of days. His magnetism, insistence, abuse, and Biblical interpretation led to disastrous consequences to those who followed him and the authorities who would pen him in.

How we read this strange book at the end of the Bible has vital importance. Revelation is not a code to be unlocked. It won't reveal predictions to crack the stock market. It won't help you make sense of strange happenstances in history. It won't reveal the moment or year

---

11 Carolyn Harris, "The Murder of Rasputin."

12 Revelation 5:1–2

13 "The Book of Koresh," *Newsweek*, October 10, 1993, https://www.newsweek.com/book-koresh-194344

or day when Jesus will come back. The authors of the New Testament expected Jesus to come back "like a thief in the night,"[14] at any given moment. But we continue to live in the gaping maw of history, the here and the not yet, the expectation that Jesus changes everything, but the pressing reality that the world is seemingly broken beyond repair. This is exactly the promise lurking under Revelation—God *persists*. God's love persists through all that the world could muster for these ancient Christians. And God's love will persist in our seasons of pandemic, discord, wars and rumors of wars, economic disparity, political polarization, and more.

REVELATION IS NOT A MANUAL FOR THE END OF THE WORLD

I love myself an IKEA manual. Open that blue-printed delight, and I can build anything. I've never been all that handy. But give me an obscure Swedish title, some aluminum screws, and a stack of fiberboard, and I'll grab the nearest Allen wrench to fill a house with furniture. They're brilliant, those manuals. No words because they ship them all over the world. A few carefully drawn images, step-by-step instructions, smiling sketch people, and voila, anyone is a carpenter.

One of the most common misconceptions of Revelation is that it is a manual for the end of the world. Folks think that Jesus will return in exactly the way that it is outlined in Revelation. So if we are on the lookout, we might catch the first or second movements of the play and anticipate the rest of the story. Using this reasoning, the strange beasts described in the middle of Revelation can start to look a bit like hulking tanks or swarming fighter jets. Like one of those Magic Eye puzzles, if you blur your vision just right, you'll start to see something lurking underneath the patterns and images.

The *Left Behind* series cemented contemporary imagination of Revelation as a blueprint for Armageddon. Stylized as a fiction series, *Left Behind* begins with the rapture, a moment when all "true

---

14 1 Thessalonians 5:2; Revelation 16:15

believers" are whisked away to heaven while the rest of the world is left behind to face a time of tribulation filled with famine, war, persecution, world order, and countless anti-Semitic tropes. *Left Behind* is an action-novel series with video game franchises and film adaptations, the most recent of which premiered in 2023. The sixteen-book series sold eighty million copies worldwide. For reference, that's nearly as many copies as the *Game of Thrones* series, which sold ninety million. Published between 1995 and 2007, *Left Behind* imagined the turn of the millennium as a reenactment of the book of Revelation, though surprisingly few details line up with the text we are studying together. Written with all of the special effects of a summer Hollywood blockbuster, it models and normalizes a specific interpretation of Revelation that is a relatively recent innovation.

The basic premise of the title—the so-called rapture—is actually a misinterpretation of a text outside of Revelation. Nowhere in the apocalyptic book at the end of the Bible is there any concept that only true believers will be whisked away to heaven and a remnant will remain on earth.[15] Rapture theology is not tied to the vast centuries of historical Christian teaching, emerging instead somewhere around 1830 for the first time. A part of a specific thread of fundamentalism (dispensational premillennialism for the curious), this theology interprets some prophecies in the Bible as unfulfilled. It purports that the church is awaiting the coming of a new epoch inaugurated by Christ's return and will then follow a script outlined in Revelation. In the 1830s, John Nelson Darby formalized the theology in Ireland, and it was spread widely through the growth of the fundamentalist movement in the United States between 1910 and 1930. If history is not your jam, this means that Americans weren't holding these ideas, hearing them from pulpits, or reading them in books and pamphlets until my grandmother was born. As part of the centuries

---

15 I understand that this may be a leap (of faith) for some who were raised in a rapture tradition. I don't argue the full point here to focus our time on what Revelation actually has to say to us. To find more, read Barbara Rossing's *The Rapture Exposed: The Message of Hope in the Book of Revelation*.

of Christian interpretation and tradition, the concept of the rapture is an outlier, a newcomer. Perhaps better described as a noxious weed, rapture theology has led to some incredibly hurtful and disastrous interpretations of Revelation.

When I first remember opening the pages of Revelation, I imagined it as a comic book that almost didn't need the technicolor drawings alongside. The images leap off the page. Glassy seas and bowls of wrath. Horsemen, and dragons, and plagues, oh my! As a younger child, I don't think I took it too seriously. It never came up in Sunday school. There were few Revelation passages on my list to memorize from parochial school. But I did have an early imagination for Armageddon.

In the late 1990s and early 2000s there was a run on apocalyptic films. My favorite starred Bruce Willis as a rough-and-tumble oil driller who was called upon by NASA and the president of the United States to save the world from an asteroid on course to destroy the planet. Not quite the Christmas playlist of *Die Hard*, but *Armageddon* is a classic. Its tear-jerking ballad, wailed by Aerosmith's Steven Tyler, was on every slow dance playlist of my adolescence and accompanied my first crush. For a few years it seemed like every other blockbuster was about a major weather event, comet, volcano, or perfect storm threatening to destroy our way of life. Looking back on these movies, many of them look cheesy. They suspend the disbelief of the audience long enough to nearly destroy the world, then pull us back into reality and a universe that preserves our way of life.

In some ways, the predictability of these films gets a little closer to the genre of Revelation than a manual for the end of the world. Just like I knew that Liv Tyler and Ben Affleck would survive *Armageddon*, the ancients for whom John wrote Revelation would have heard resonances all over this book. They would have understood the way it danced through every corner of Hebrew Scripture. They would have anticipated the points made about Jesus. They would have felt in their bones images and references that have eroded throughout the generations. In order for us to overhear the promises whispering from even the scariest corners of Revelation, we'll need to unlearn our imagination of Revelation as a blueprint for the end of the world and a code to be deciphered. It may come as a disappointment because we won't be starring in the latest Dan Brown (or *Left Behind*) mystery. All in all, however, we'll begin to hear promises that can ground our hope in love that lit the stars.

WHAT IS SCRIPTURE?

When teaching the Bible to folks in our congregation and in other settings, I've come up with a working definition of Scripture. It makes sure that I'm not *just* sharing all deconstruction, all the "nos" about what the Bible isn't. For all of the ways that the Bible has left me bruised and rashy, it is also a source of great love and inspiration and trust and possibility. It's the book that I've wrestled with the most. It's the book that has kept me up at night. It's the book that continues to call out to me wherever I bump up against it. My working definition of Scripture helps ground me in an awareness of how this book has a hold on me. It helps me clarify how I want to learn from it. And it helps me understand how my perspective is different from folks I bump into. I don't expect my definition to become yours. Perhaps, instead, it helps you ask questions about how you have come to understand Scripture, how you've been taught to interpret it, and how you might want to move toward understanding its role in your life. My definition is fairly straightforward: *Scripture is our witness to the living voice of God.*

I no longer defend Scripture as infallible or inerrant, but I've settled into other adjectives including inspired. The Bible has been painstakingly translated, studied, written by hand, annotated, hidden under floorboards, prayed, sung, wrestled and reckoned with. It's been seen on stage and screen. And it is ours. It's not (only) mine. I don't have any claim over the right or only interpretation of this strange book. I'm a part of a wide stream of traditions—Christian, Jewish, and otherwise—that have wrestled with various stories over centuries and millennia. Even though I've walked away from the particular approach to Christian faith that formed me, Evangelical folks have just as much of a right to interpret and talk about this book as I do (though some may disagree with the last part of that statement). It's ours.

It is a witness to something beyond what we can taste or touch or feel on a daily basis. Scripture asks questions that other books don't quite scratch at. It calls us to ponder our purpose on this planet, reminds us of the generations who came long before us, and reimagines narratives that could easily slip by forgotten. I believe that it points us to the *living voice of God*. Certainly directed at those of us English majors whose hearts pitter-patter at typographical references, the United Church of Christ had an advertising campaign a few years ago with a giant comma. It read, "Never place a period where God put a comma." God is still speaking, through our conversations, through our investigations, through our curiosity and wrestling. By contending with Scripture, especially in the company of others, we are listening for the living voice of God, speaking in our company, whispering promises that our ancestors heard clearly, indicting us for challenges they couldn't have imagined, bringing us to faith and pointing us outward toward a world that longs for good news. God's voice is alive and well in the person of Jesus, the events that took place two millennia ago, and the ongoing work of the Spirit as we wrestle with these ancient texts that have been preserved and interpreted by our ancestors in faith. Revelation is part of our Scripture, and, though we might prefer otherwise, we need to wrestle with it so that other fringe interpreters don't speak the only line on center stage.

If my definition of Scripture works for you, fabulous. If it is different from yours or helps you start to think about how you might write your own, even better.

2

What Revelation Is

At the beginning of each chapter, I offer you an invitation to read Revelation. My hope is that you will read from the actual pages of an actual Bible. Virtual is fine, but I prefer opening up a hard, soft, or leather-bound tome with a pencil in hand. I like to underline words that jump out to me, put question marks next to particularly odd sections, or write notes in the margins from things I find elsewhere. I invite you to do the same, slowly reading a book that might feel intimidating or troublesome or out of touch. If you can read even portions of Revelation with some understanding, you can go anywhere else in Scripture. So let's go! We need not look any further than the first few verses of Revelation to find out what it is. We'll walk through Revelation 1:1–20 and listen to the way that this text describes itself. Rather than a code to unlock or a blueprint to follow, we'll find a prophecy, a letter, and an apocalypse.

REVELATION TELLS US WHAT IT IS

Enough is enough. Let's read the damn (I feel like I'm allowed this curse because of the text we're studying together) book, shall we? If you've been patient enough to read an introduction and a first chapter that is pretty close to a second introduction, kudos. I'm not sure my ADHD brain could have.

Revelation actually tells us what it is in the first few verses. One thing you should know about the Bible is that none of the books originally included the titles that they are given in the highlighted and frayed handbook or coffee table artifact you have in front of you. Whether you memorized the order of these books at Bible camp or need to look at the table of contents every time to find a page in the Scriptures, the titles in our modern-day Bibles were added long after the books were written.

Many of the letters in the New Testament are written to the audience named in the letter: Romans to an early Christian community in Rome; Corinthians to a gathering of Jesus-followers in Corinth. You get the idea. Many are written by Paul; others are suspected by most scholars to be written by students of Paul, or people who wanted to borrow Paul's name for a boost in authority. A few additional letters, called the Catholic letters, are named after the authors—James, Peter, John, and Jude. The Gospels are each titled after the traditional author, two of whom (Matthew and John), tradition would often have it, heard the words right from Jesus' mouth. According to tradition, Mark and Luke received the witness from Peter and Paul, who heard it right from Jesus. New Testament scholarship teaches us that the Gospels were likely written a full generation after Jesus. Luke writes an orange sticky-note (Luke's favorite Astrobright color is definitely orange) at the top of his gospel to an intended purpose and audience ("most excellent Theophilus"). John opens with a cosmic poem (surely in blue Astrobright) that sounds an awful lot like the story of creation in Genesis. Matthew begins with a genealogy inspired by the family trees throughout Genesis and other Old Testament texts (yellow, for the record). Mark gets right into the action (red). That leaves us with two outliers in the New Testament, namely Hebrews and Revelation.

Hebrews contains perhaps the finest Greek of all of the New Testament. It is unlikely that it was written by Paul and is decidedly not a letter. Paul wrote to specific audiences with fiery challenge, hopeful affirmation, bits of poetry, and early hymns of Jesus. While his letters are often the source material of doctrine, dogma, faith, and fundamentals, they were not intended to be a formula of faith. They were intended for the community that received them, offering pastoral advice, reminders of the living Christ, and affirmations of the Spirit's work among them. But back to Hebrews. Most scholars agree that Hebrews is a sermon of sorts, and its title comes from the suspected intended audience, the Hebrews. It translates the message of Jesus's life, death, and resurrection using inherited symbols from Jewish ritual.

Revelation's title is drawn from the opening words of the book: "The Revelation of Jesus Christ."[1] Revelation is a translation of the Greek word *apokalypsis,* meaning unveiling. I bet you can figure out what words we get from this Greek word. If you can't, I'll spell it out for you. I am a C. I am a C-H. I am . . . just kidding. It's *apocalypse.* In full, this strange book at the end of the Bible is called *A Revelation of Jesus Christ.* Just a verse later, the author (John) writes, "Blessed is the one who reads the words of *prophecy,*"[2] which leads us to our next clue. Revelation is a prophecy. And just one sentence after that, we see the traditional beginning of a letter, much like those from Paul or James or Jude: "John to the seven churches that are in Asia."[3]

In short, Revelation tells us right away what it is. It is a prophecy. It is a letter. And it is an *apokalypsis*—an apocalypse, a revelation, an unveiling.

A PROPHET AND A PROPHECY

Let's start with the prophecy part. Prophets encounter the word of God in their bones. Through word or vision or symbol or art, prophets embody the immediacy of God's call in the world. They *hear* or *witness* the living voice of God firsthand. Moses took off his sandals

---

1 Revelation 1:1
2 Revelation 1:3
3 Revelation 1:4

when he approached the burning bush because he knew that God was near. Isaiah was brought up to the throne-room of God, where strange six-winged creatures called seraphim put hot coals to his lips to wipe his sin away. Ezekiel ate a scroll and was carried to a valley full of dry bones brought to life by the words God spoke through him.

Revelation is an ecstatic vision that the author, John of Patmos, describes in the pages that follow. We don't know what the vision experience felt like. Did John fall asleep and dream these strange images? Was he active in the process? Could he wander around and search the space, or was it presented to him? Was it intoxicating? Terrifying? Did it startle him out of sleep with pulse pounding and sweat on his brow? John is clearly an active part of the vision, responding with emotions that range as far as the visions—fear, sadness, joy, longing, and anger. When John first sees the scroll with seven seals, for example, he "began to weep bitterly because no one was found worthy to open the scroll or to look into it."[4] John is part of the vision, not simply recording something that appears on a projection in front of him. He is connected to it, responding with it, and inviting readers to do the same.

People often doubt these sorts of spiritual encounters with the divine. We might be willing to read about them from ancients, but these days we rarely allow space for people to articulate experiences that extend beyond our imagination. But the prophet's experience of the prophecy is an essential component to encountering the words on the page. Revelation has a physical tenacity to it, leaping off the page through the expressions that John shares. He actively explores the images that unfold throughout the book, looking around at what he sees, carried up to tall mountains, witnessing God's city descend from the heavens, overlooking a glassy sea that shimmers like precious gems, enraptured by a heavenly choir that sings without ceasing, terrified by the hold that beasts have on creation, and much more. John's storytelling may take a little getting used to. He doesn't linger on his emotions as long as contemporary writers might. John doesn't say what it feels like to be "in the Spirit." He doesn't sound

---

4 Revelation 5:4

the melody of the songs sung, but instead captures words. Rather, John spends time describing the vision, reaching to analogies that ancient people would clearly understand, connecting his witness to the stories of Scripture in the Hebrew Bible, and inviting all of us into the unfolding narrative. John was caught up in an ecstatic, imaginative encounter with God that left him with a message to share.[5]

Next, we don't know how John recorded his prophetic experience into words. Was he like a songwriter, caught in a feverish moment of inspiration, writing couplets and chords late into the night? Did John receive the vision first, then take time to carefully write it down, recalling other passages from Scripture? Did he carefully rehearse it, revising and revisiting visions? We don't know. However, the author of this odd book of the Bible has agency and voice and perspective. He uses the language and the references at his disposal, recalling stories from his spiritual ancestors, connecting contemporary references, and shaping a vision that would speak to specific churches in his community. We are left with the text, full of images, visions, quotations, songs, and a heartbeat that pulses across every page. There is a persistent hope lurking even in the scariest corners of these verses. It leaps out, startling me with possibility and potential.

We've been trained to think of the word *prophecy* as a prediction. Somehow prophets see the future and share it to the world so that we might anticipate a miracle to come. There is a group of books in the Old Testament known as the prophetic books. Some are long (Isaiah and Ezekiel, for example). These are known as the major prophets. It's not that they're more important or influential—just longer. The minor prophets are, *you guessed it*, shorter books. They include Malachi, Hezekiah, Jonah, and Micah. These shorter books are no less important, just simply fewer chapters and verses, which is why some Hebrew Bible teachers prefer to follow the Jewish naming that binds them into one Book of the Twelve.

---

5 If you are curious about the ecstatic, experiential side of Revelation, read John Pilch and Bruce Melina's *A Social Science Commentary on Revelation*.

Whenever I teach the prophetic books, people want to know exactly how they predict the coming of the Messiah, Jesus, who of course we Christians want to hear all about. But if we limit our discussion of prophets to predicting the future, we are missing another story entirely. For the ancients, and for many contemporary Jews, the prophetic books are not at all about predicting the future. Rather, the prophetic books call God's people back to faithfulness. The prophets embolden and embody an alternative imagination for life here on earth.

There are plenty of people who comb through the pages of Revelation, making strange calculations, drawing odd conclusions, and occasionally convincing many people that they've cracked the code. But, as we've discussed, Revelation isn't a code to be cracked or a manual for the end of the world. The prophetic call of Revelation reaches back to the calls for justice from the Hebrew prophets and draws a line in the sand, insisting that the followers of Jesus remember their call in the world and maintain their unique identity, just as the most powerful force in the world (Rome) insists on fitting their mold.

REMEMBER WHO YOU ARE

When my eldest daughter was three, she had a series of favorite bedtime books. They were never the most compelling or had the best artwork. I have several of them still memorized—a pouty ocean creature, snoring roadwork equipment, and even a crayon revolution. But one (and maybe only one) of the stories still brings tears to my eyes. She called it "Daddy's favorite book." Perhaps because it was my favorite, she wanted to hear it more—Maurice Sendak's *Where the Wild Things Are*. We've read it thousands of times, and it hasn't lost an ounce of its magic. We romp and roar and revel in the cadence and the sketches. When I was asked to give the graduate address at our local high school, I chose to preach using *Where the Wild Things Are*. I connected the wild things to the new creatures that students would encounter—new challenges, new people, new roars and rhythms.

Sendak's imagination of time was easy for parents to understand as they sent their children off on new adventures, remembering only a breath ago when they were walking for the first time. The graduates leaned in when I shared Max's magic trick of silencing the monsters they might encounter, stilling their spirits, and hearing the still voice of the divine among them. And I'm certain I saw a few tears when I reiterated that all students could make their way back to their very own room, where supper would be waiting for them, and it would still be hot. There is something accessible about a good bedtime story, no matter how old we are, something that deepens breath and settles fluttering heartbeats. In a few brief sentences and splashes of color on the page, we let go of the heartbreaks of today and dare once again to dream about tomorrow.

In some ways Scripture can function like a bedtime story, with dog-eared pages, plot points avoided or reframed for the moment at hand, favorite characters with imaginative voicing, and a sense of place in the world and in the cosmos. Like the in-between moment of bedtime, Scripture straddles the here and the not yet, the memories of our ancestors and the hopes of generations yet to come. In the words of the prophet Joel, "our elders will have visions and your youth will dream dreams."[6]

In the middle of the biggest book of the Bible, Psalms, there is a beautiful poem that I imagine just like a favorite bedtime story. On a late summer night with children who defer bedtime for *just one more* story, a weary storyteller beckons benediction with these words:

"Give ear, O my people, to my teaching;
incline your ears to the words of my mouth.
I will open my mouth in a parable;
I will utter dark sayings from of old,
things that we have heard and known,
that our ancestors have told us."[7]

---

6 Joel 2:28; Acts 2:17
7 Psalm 78:1–2

Restless children settle into seats, listening carefully for their favorite characters in the story of their ancestors, pondering anew what the "great deeds of the Lord" might be, dreaming of their own stories and how God might work new possibilities in them.

The narrative of Scripture repeatedly calls the people to remember who they are, the covenant made with God and humanity, naming ways they have been complicit in the brokenness of the world and inspiring them to live differently. Certain passages of the Bible just stir the imagination—"Dark sayings from of old." Mysterious flames sparked by our ancestors and carefully tended by elders and children alike. These mysteries contain wisdom and gift, adventure and promise, challenge and indictment. The storyteller recalls "the wondrous deeds the Lord has done," not as a historian reciting facts, but applying their meaning to the situation of the moment.

"Never let the truth get in the way of a good story," said Mark Twain. Various verses of Scripture disagree about timelines, the results of specific battles, which powerful figure was moral or noble, and who was on the underside of victory. For those of us who grew up in fundamentalisms of various kinds, any apparent disagreement in the Bible will grind our gears. Entire circular logics are built around the notion that the Scriptures are inerrant, without error. But the reality is that the verses of the Bible are not always tuned in perfect harmony. They don't speak with one voice, but from a chorus of voices from different angles and vantage points and moments in time and space. The storyteller from the Psalms, like John recounting Revelation, is after truth, but a contextual, pondering truth that applies in this moment differently than it did for the generation previous and the generation before that. It's a truth that emerges in the questioning and wrestling and interpreting of Scripture, rather than a timeless interpretation distilled into static dogma. The Bible shares memories, a set of stories from Genesis and beyond. But it interprets and reinterprets and invites all of us to become interpreters, a community of storytellers, speaking from our diverse voices and vantage points a vision of love that lit the stars.

Revelation is addressing the challenges of the moment—an early Jesus movement meeting in houses and public spaces under fear of persecution and death. It dreams a vision that challenges the authority of Rome—a military superpower and an economic engine that left little room for difference or contribution from those outside the halls of power. The followers of a zealous rabbi threatened to unsettle the assumed religious and economic power of the empire because they did not submit. But Revelation's source material comes from the shared memory of the Scriptures—largely the prophetic books, inviting that early entourage to see their challenges tied to a story that stretches far before them and will last far beyond.

WRESTLING WITH CORPORATE MEMORY

I had a friend once ask me to tell her a story that says something about who I am. She was asking me to share a memory, a moment that was informative somehow of the person that I was becoming. In this liminal, in-between moment in my life, I remember testing her with the memory that I chose, filtering through the surprising, confusing, strange memories in my life and landing on a scene from childhood when I looked up at the stars on the roof of the chicken coop in our back yard. Our memories shape our personalities, the things we're willing to try or risk, the way we view ourselves and the world. As an only child, I've often felt like the only keeper of my family memories. My spouse is the eldest of five children. I can tell countless stories from her childhood because I've heard them tossed back and forth between siblings in the beautiful banter of adults who share lives with one another. But sharing a memory is a tricky thing. Who gets to tell the story? And from what vantage point? The eldest siblings might laugh about a story of playing *Cool Runnings* and sending the younger siblings careening down the driveway in a Red Flyer wagon. But the youngest quickly chime in with the pain of the skinned knee and the tears as they ran to tell mom.

We are having an important conversation about corporate memory as a culture right now. Just as the decision of who gets to tell the story from childhood, we wrestle in public with choices of who gets to tell the story of our life together as a community, a nation, or a world. *Remembering* has significant political implications. Who gets to choose what and how we remember various aspects of our shared history? How do we share our memories with the next generation? Who gets to tell the stories? In his podcast, *Revisionist History*, Malcolm Gladwell revisits "overlooked or misunderstood" artifacts from history, examining from a different angle plot points many have inherited without interrogation. In one applicable episode, Gladwell asks why we insist that lapses in memory are gaps in moral character. "Free Brian Williams" messes with our understanding of the accuracy of memory by using the example of Brian Williams, who told a war story on national television that didn't happen as he described it. Exploring scientific research in memory, Gladwell forces us to question the ways that we remember so-called facts of history and invites us to see a more nuanced view of the way we share collective memory. Our memories are shaped just as much by the stories that we tell as they are by the apparent "facts" on the ground.

The 1619 Project uses long-form journalism to reframe American history by centering the narrative on the year that the first people were forcibly removed from their African homelands to build an economy on unpaid enslaved labor on the North American continent. In our polarized environment it sparked book banning and teacher censorship, perhaps because it touches on one of the most profound questions of our American narrative, a sacred story of our origins. Founded on what many have called the original sin of slavery, America is rather seen as a deeply flawed experiment still in the throes of understanding its own brokenness and the way it has built systems and structures around domination rather than opportunity. It might be easy to look back into the annals of history to find examples of empirical might and oppression (and we'll find them in Revelation), but it is entirely different to look at our neighborhoods and deeds, highways and corporate structures, elementary schools and universities, seeing how they reek of racism, privilege, and white supremacy. It has proven too tough a pill to swallow for many in our shared world.

Prophetic texts call the people back to who they are, but not in a static or nostalgic dream of what *used to be*. Rather the prophetic books cast an alternative imagination for what is possible. I had a professor once say that there are two ways to inspire change—a burning platform or a glorious vision. A burning platform indicts people with the enormity and urgency of a problem—if we don't fix this now, there may not be a tomorrow. A glorious vision beckons people into an imagination of a world where the problems of the day are completely eclipsed by the envisioned possibilities. Prophetic books use both approaches through harsh visions of judgment and stunning dreams of possibility.

HARSH VISIONS OF JUDGMENT

I grew up with a preacher who often got angry from the pulpit. We worshipped in a small, simple church on the outskirts of town. It had a tall white steeple that seemed a bit out of place, like an afterthought on a graham cracker house at Christmas, stuck to the top with a little extra frosting. Outside the church there was an enormous oak tree. I remember Easter sunrise services around a fire pit, guitar chords strumming softly and singing old Vineyard and camp tunes. Even as I try to remember, I can't recall any of the subjects of his sermons. I can't remember stories or illustrations or even various Bible passages that he would use. But I remember the anger, the pounding fists and reddened face. It's an anger I've since seen in political rallies and quasi-religious nationalistic festivals. It formed a reaction in me every time I opened the Bible. I expected that it was shouting at me, pounding its fists with righteous anger. It took me quite some time to get over this response, only to find myself in a tradition that much prefers to find the cozy, sickly sweet, always endearing corners of the Bible.

My friend Dr. Michael Chan is a scholar of the Hebrew Bible and has helped me understand how essential some of this judgment really is. Often we are lulled into a space of reluctant apathy. The world around us is impossible to get our hands around, so why would we resist? Why would we live otherwise? Why would we dare to dream something different? Visions of judgment cut through the apathy and hold a mirror up to our own complicity in the malfunctions of a world gone wrong. Dr. Chan says that judgment frees us from our delusions. We may be deluded on one hand that nothing we do can make an impact. Or we might try to change everything with our ego, only to make an entirely different set of mistakes. Michael has helped me heal old wounds about judgment, damnation, and working my own salvation out in fear and trembling. Because judgment always felt like I was stuck in the third row of that old church listening to an angry preacher. There was nowhere to turn, only the knowledge that I was flawed, broken, full of sin, and perhaps even worthless. But judgment can be freedom, depending on the space we occupy.

From my corner in the third row of our small church, I could see the heating duct that I would hide in during youth group midnight games of hide-and-seek. (No one ever found me. Best spot ever!) When the preacher was yelling, it was as if I were stuck in the heating duct, unable to move, feeling the scratches of fiberglass insulation itching eternally for a theology that struck me and others down for who we are. As Dr. Chan has described it to me, the prophetic words of God's judgment shake us out of our own self-delusion. They reform habits and practices that have become stuck. They call us out of a stagnant apathy into freedom because they call the systems and structures and habits what they are—misguided assumptions that go all the way back to the beginning.

It reminds me of a strange story from the book of Genesis about the Tower of Babel. It is near the bottom of a long spiral of humanity falling into brokenness. In a stitched-together narrative of strange bedtime stories, Genesis gathers a people and reminds them who they are while they are living in exile. Away from home, they might lose their identity, tradition, ritual, all the things that made them family. The story says the people built a tower reaching all the way to the heavens, so that they could look God in the eye and perhaps be just as the serpent suggested, "like God." In order to build this tower, they all spoke exactly the same language, consolidating the beautiful tapestry that God created into one language. Humans, in their attempt to build a structure and take over God's role as sustainer of all things, actually bend the gifts of creation to meet their own needs, ignoring the promises and blessings inherent in the goodness with which God blesses creation.

Revelation brings John to the very heights of heaven, into the throne-room of God, but there is never any question of John becoming "like God." Rather, Revelation shows the powers that rebel against God for what they are, distortions of the vision that God has for humanity. Through its terrifying visions, Revelation will wake us up from our apathy and insist on an embodied resistance to the powers that rebel against God's vision of wholeness, God's dreams of possibility for all of creation.

STUNNING DREAMS OF POSSIBILITY

I spent a summer on the south shore of the largest inland freshwater sea on the planet: Lake Superior. We led young people through week-long excursions into the wilderness and would often spend one final night on the beach of this Great Lake. On rainless nights, we would sleep under the stars. Without tides, the waves are only made by wind blowing from Canada. I have seen the lake like glass, and I have seen it throw surfboard-worthy eight-foot swells.

Every time I spent the night on the shore of that lake, I would wake up slightly before sunrise. The sky would deepen in color, neither darker or lighter, more of a depth of color. My friend Pastor Natalia Terfa preached a beautiful sermon once about the fact that she despises the famous line, "It's always darkest before the dawn." She's right, it's not darkest right before the dawn. The color does change, however. It hints at the pyrotechnics that will come with the sunrise, but it doesn't quite show its hand. With a good poker face, the sky over Gitchi Gummi almost seemed to stretch beyond the horizon.

An ancient song of the church[8] calls it the dayspring—the first light of the morning that sparks the colorful palette of daylight. The Psalmist similarly envisions "rising on the wings of the morning."[9] There is something truly magical about a sunrise from beginning to end. It has always reminded me of the possibilities of each day, each turn of our corporate sphere an opportunity for something else. The prophetic books articulate dreams of something new peeking around the corner, deepening the colors of night, sparking fire at sunrise, and calling us into a new thing.

Revelation articulates stunning visions of possibility at every turn. It's easy to spend time in the scary bits, and we will certainly thumb through them. But the beautiful visions are enough to keep you engaged through every page. The first few verses of poetry draw us in:

> Then I turned to see whose voice it was that spoke to me, and on turning I saw seven golden lampstands, and in the midst of the lampstands I saw one like the Son of Man, clothed with a long robe and with a golden sash across his chest. His head and his hair were white as white wool, white as snow; his eyes were like a flame of fire; his feet were like burnished bronze, refined as in a furnace, and his voice was like the sound of many waters. In his right hand he held seven stars, and from his mouth came a sharp, two-edged sword, and his face was like the sun shining with full force.[10]

I know I have heard the sound of many waters, the multiplicity of its voices. Water doesn't speak with one voice; it clatters and shifts and changes. Like the shore of Lake Superior, sometimes it is soft, lapping quietly, while other times it is the only thing you can hear.

---

8 The Great O Antiphons, if you are curious, are more commonly known through our hymn, "O Come, O Come Emmanuel." Using seven (a number we'll get to soon!) images, each hymn uses a different metaphor to sing what the birth of Christ means for the world.

9 Psalm 139:9, NIV

10 Revelation 1:12–16

Rivers too speak differently at different moments. They bubble and swirl, rush and roar, glide and glisten. These visions help us not only to hear the living voice of Jesus from the pages of John's vision but to understand characteristics of Christ in the descriptors he is using. Many of them are distilled through time and space and culture, but some of them speak just as clearly today as they did yesterday. We can all imagine the sound of many waters. We can envision the wings of the morning. We can see the flicker of a candle flame.

John is clear about the challenges. He "share[s] the persecution and the kingdom and the endurance in Jesus."[11] John is exiled on an island called Patmos for his confession of Jesus. He is separated from his community, writing letters in the opening section of the book to seven churches scattered across contemporary Turkey. John is a political prisoner, exiled by the Roman authorities, and by the text we have, perhaps for explicitly political prophecy that was a threat to Roman rule. One of my favorite factoids is that John may have been exiled because of practicing *magic*, which was categorized in the same way as prophecy, whether Jewish, Christian, or otherwise.

Like the prophetic texts of the Hebrew Bible, Revelation alternates between stunning visions and harsh judgments, sometimes in the same breath. As contemporary readers it is sometimes hard to follow. Instead of the advice of my leadership professor to provide *either* a burning platform *or* a glorious vision, prophetic texts give both. In some ways, it depends on which side of the coin you view things from.

Every year, many of us gather to hear one of the great orations of our shared history—Martin Luther King Jr.'s dream that America might live up to its promises and make good on the check it has already written to embody a place and a people where freedom will ring. Some of us may hear clearly the tenor of Dr. King's voice rising, consonants exploding with a quotation from the prophet Amos: "But let justice roll down like waters and righteousness like an ever flowing stream."[12] We hear already the promise in this statement, the vision of

---

11 Revelation 1:9
12 Amos 5:24

justice flowing like a mighty river. But Dr. King certainly brought with it also the vision of judgment that precedes this line: "I hate, I despise your festivals, and I take no delight in your solemn assemblies."[13] Dr. King certainly wielded both burning platform and glorious vision. Just a few months earlier, in April 1963, Dr. King wrote from the Birmingham Jail of white moderates who turned the gospel into something otherworldly rather than a clarion call for justice here and now:

> I have watched white churches stand on the sideline and merely mouth pious irrelevancies and sanctimonious trivialities. I have watched so many churches commit themselves to a completely other-worldly religion which made a strange distinction between body and soul, the sacred and the secular.[14]

As a white moderate, the waters of justice are waters of destruction. The vision from Amos decries lazy, solemn assemblies that loft their heads in the clouds only to ignore persistent oppression on the ground. In Revelation, Jesus speaks with a tongue that is a two-edged sword. It cuts both ways, providing freedom and judgment in the same moment.

Oddly enough, some of the same white moderate churches, now perhaps white conservative churches, turn Revelation into an otherworldly text that stirs visions of the afterlife while ignoring its consistent rhythm of concern for the here and now. An obsession with distilling prediction from this prophecy too conveniently dodges the slice of this sword that cuts at the apathy of many white churches.

UNRESTRAINED ACT OF IMAGINATION

I've gotten to know a little bit one of the elders of biblical studies, criticism, and imagination. Walter Brueggemann entered the pandemic at the ripe age of 87, writing regularly for the blog I help lead,

---

13 Amos 5:21
14 Martin Luther King, Jr. "Letter from Birmingham Jail."

Church Anew. His spirit and wisdom and voice are a testimony to the way that the Bible can remain fresh, relevant, and compelling. From his home in Michigan, he sends weekly reflections on ways that the biblical text intersects with our shared American story—politics, economics, sports, contemporary events, and the concerns of parents as they shape the minds and spirits of the next generation.

In one of his most influential books, Brueggemann speaks of a *Prophetic Imagination,* an alternative reality called forth by the power of divine expression, memory, and vision. First published in 1978, the book preaches as well today as it did nearly a half-century ago. Brueggemann draws from the Scriptures to awaken the American church from its slumber "with little power to believe or act,"[15] to help it remember the roots of its proclamation, and use the Scriptures as a way to call it forward. Drawing from the tradition, shared memory from the Bible, and the unruly imagination of the Holy Spirit, Brueggemann evokes an alternative imagination and forms an alternative consciousness by criticizing and energizing—burning platform and glorious vision. Tearing down foundations through deconstruction and carefully stitching together a more expansive vision of faith. *The Prophetic Imagination* uses the story of Moses, the royal tradition, the counter narratives of the Hebrew prophets, and the witness of Jesus in the gospels as source material.

With Revelation, the imagination knows no boundaries and is unveiled before our very eyes through unrestrained acts of imagination. In a piece for the *Church Anew* blog, Brueggemann applied his characteristic interpretation to the book of Revelation:

> For all our misconstruals of the book, the Book of Revelation is a severe, unrestrained act of imagination that traces out a world that is alternative to the stratified world of the Roman Empire that has reduced everyone to a commodity, and that refuses the wondrous freedom and generosity of genuine community. This

---

15 Walter Brueggemann, *The Prophetic Imagination,* second edition (Minneapolis: Fortress Press, 2001), 1.

vision in the Book of Revelation is neither "other-worldly" escapism nor is it about life after death. It is rather an act of insistent imagination that competes with and resists the imposing world of Rome. (In our context, that world is now articulated through limitless capitalist greed and unrestrained white supremacy.)[16]

If Revelation tells us it is a prophecy, it draws us into its *unrestrained act of imagination*. It unveils a world that stands in stark opposition to the forces of its day and invites comparisons with the oppressive regimes in our time. It draws us in through song and deep longing, fiery drama, and bountiful visions. Revelation uses harsh visions of judgment and stunning dreams of possibility to form an alternative imagination for a people that couldn't envision a way forward. It makes possible what might not be possible for ancient Jesus followers and perhaps for us today as well. But before we start to see the vision, we have to begin to claim the soil we're standing on, understanding our own vantage point within this oracle.

MY INHERITANCE

Naming the theologies and inheritances that are no longer helpful to each of us or our community is an essential task of reading ancient Scripture. Reading Revelation forces us to take a critical examination, a fearless moral inventory, of the baggage of our tradition. You've already received some of my own confessions of a white American Evangelical, reflecting the ways that I have encountered Revelation in the world. Throughout the coming chapters I want to invite you to look at the ideas you've inherited about Scripture from family upbringing, various church traditions, and popular culture.

Our theological inheritance matters. My colleague Peter is a pastor's kid (lovingly called a PK) who grew up in the Lutheran tradition.

---

16 Walter Brueggemann, "A Music-Making Counter Community," *Church Anew*, July 19, 2023.

He traveled throughout the world while his dad served in Israel and the Middle East. While we were teaching together, we explored the theme of grace, how it is a gift to understand that God already tends our souls, our spirits, and all that is in us. I remember looking at him, astonished. He never had a moment in his life when he questioned or doubted that God loved him and cared for him. He never had a moment of doubt that his salvation was in question. This was not the theological tradition that I was raised in, where there were constant temptations, persistent detours that could pull you away from God's love and presence. Peter's imagination for what God is doing in the Scriptures is informed by the embodied knowledge that God loves and cares for Peter always. Mine is informed by seeking grace and trying to believe it with every ounce of my being.

Next, our social location matters. Elizabeth Schüssler Fiorenza wrote an incredible commentary on Revelation, where she outlines the importance of social location in our readings of this ancient text. "Context is as important as text. What we see depends on where we stand." She shares how Revelation is a text written from the margins because John was a political prisoner being persecuted by the largest economic and military power of the world. Revelation has been marginalized by Christian tradition, which often relegates it to obscurity, ignores it, or diminishes it. And, Revelation has a powerful and important word for those living on the margins. For a people experiencing oppression, Revelation can be a breath of fresh air, where the oppressors face justice and God consistently defends those on the underside of history. For people in power, it can be a threat.

In many ways, I'm writing as someone with incredible privilege as a white, upper-middle-class, formerly Evangelical, graduate school-educated, white male. As Revelation cuts with the two-edged sword, I am often the voice of power rather than the voice on the margins. I need to wrestle with questions like:

- What does it look like for me to take seriously the harsh words of judgment that shake me from my apathy?

- How can I understand the challenging visions of Revelation as words to unmask my delusions?
- How might Revelation hold up a mirror for me to the ways that I am complicit in an empire that persists beyond Babylon and Rome?

On the other side of the two-edged sword, "Other oppressed and disadvantaged Christians read Revelation contextually as political-religious typology that speaks to their own situation. Latin American or South African liberation theologies cherish Revelation's political world of vision for its prophetic indictment of exploitation and oppression as well as its sustaining vision of justice."[17] For those in marginalized communities, people experiencing exploitation or oppression, Revelation can invite an entirely different set of questions.

Whenever we read the Bible, and especially Revelation, we need to begin with a fearless moral inventory of where we stand. I will feature voices that aren't me, don't come from the same social location, and speak with different perspectives throughout the following chapters. But for now, I invite you to spend some time thinking about the social location you stand in, pondering how the imagination of Revelation might be balm or challenge in your story and circumstance.

A LETTER

It's a frequent competition in our family to choose the best greeting card for birthdays and other special occasions. My grumpy, (nearly) middle-aged, get-off-my-lawn dad bod complains about the cost, but I am always thrilled by the response when someone opens the perfect card. We've lately been reaching for the outrageous—the guffaw cards or the oversized cardboard with purple fur and googly eyes. But I

---

17 Elisabeth Schüssler Fiorenza, *Revelation: Vision of a Just World* (Minneapolis: Fortress Press, 1991) 7.

love an understated, imprinted card with a well-placed quote and a simple message inside. It was one of these cards that I opened a few months ago. For the life of me I can't remember what the card said because the inside of the envelope grabbed my attention and still sits on my desk. Right after opening the card, the lip of the envelop read, in simple sans serif, "Text less. Write more."

I can't remember the last time I sent or received a letter in the mail. Cards, absolutely. Bills, all the time. But a letter? It's a lost art form. Historians pour over every word. Lin Manuel Miranda turned letters from the American Revolution into one of the best-selling theater productions of all time, *Hamilton*. Who knows what will be left of our civilization when all the zeros and ones of our text threads have been erased from our pocket devices?

Letters are a strange thing to overhear, especially if you are not the intended recipient. And Revelation contains even stranger letters than most. In a way, we are of course the intended recipients of letters in Scripture. Although I no longer believe that the Bible is full of inerrant words written by God with a really long pencil, I do believe that God is speaking to us through these ancient texts. But in another way, we are absolutely not the intended recipients of the letters in the New Testament. Each and every one of them includes notes to the community at hand. The New Testament is nearly half letters. Once you ride the wind of the Holy Spirit through Acts, it's all letters (except Hebrews) until the last page.

Revelation tells us that it is a letter to seven churches in Asia because it begins with a salutation. This is the part of the letter that says, "Dear Grandma," or "To whom it may concern." In our biblical letters, the salutation begins with the name of the person writing it (or with some of the letters attributed to Paul, a name that the writer might reach for to support their own claims). So right after we read that Revelation is a prophecy, we dive right into the letter:

John to the seven churches that are in Asia:
     Grace to you and peace from him who is and who was and
     who is to come and from the seven spirits who are before his

throne, and from Jesus Christ, the faithful witness, the firstborn of the dead, and the ruler of the kings of the earth.[18]

Perhaps you have heard a sermon that begins with "Grace to you and peace . . ." More formal preachers will sometimes borrow from this style of New Testament letters by beginning their address to the congregation in the same way that Paul did. As John greets the churches in Asia, he is holding their specific concerns in mind, responding to their needs, answering their questions, and providing a letter that may help in some way.

True confession—I love listening in on other people's conversations. Weird? Absolutely. But it's real. While writing this book, I camped out in a number of coffee shops, usually with my ear buds dug into my skull, cranking Philip Glass and Arvo Part and Max Richter. (Apocalypse deserves a playlist of moody minimalism.) In one of my favorite spots to write, I became aware that a local gigachurch[19] would regularly gather a variety of accountability groups. Even if I've strayed from Evangelicalism, it finds me! Or maybe we have the same taste in coffee. What a conversation to overhear! A twenty-something confessed deep dark secrets of thinking lusty thoughts or touching himself for pleasure. Even more strange, he was speaking with a young woman who told him to undertake a three-month fast of pleasure. She spoke about the deeply spiritual feelings stirred while eating nothing for days at a time. She felt closest to God in those moments that she was so hungry she was

---

18 Revelation 1:4–5

19 Perhaps you've heard of a *mega*church with thousands of members, lots of programming, a big building, and a big budget. By some definitions, the large church I serve might qualify. *Giga*churches are orders of magnitude larger than the megachurches that precede them. They often feature celebrity preachers, buildings that look like black-box theaters with lights, smoke machines, lasers, and hip musicians on stage. Many of these churches livestream a sermon from their celebrity preacher into satellite buildings around a metropolitan area or around the nation.

throwing up. Maybe find a quieter spot for this conversation than a trendy coffee shop? These interactions were hard to hear and see, day after day, week after week. After the initial intrigue, I gave up and plugged the tunes back in. It left me with way too many questions. Why was this young man talking to this young woman about these issues? Was he posturing in a way? Was this like a new form of white Evangelical peacock feathers? Why did the young woman share a story that sounded like terribly disordered eating as a spiritual experience? Was this something of a practice in their church? Will she find help?

I don't want this example to come across as flippant. For many of us who have experienced this kind of manipulation in Evangelical circles, laughter is an easy coping mechanism. I live with memories like this conversation in my bones and don't revisit them frequently, but the bruises are still there. I am keenly aware that purity culture does real damage to people and to me—to our souls and our bodies. Sometimes laughter can untie the knots and the absurdity of this culture to reveal a freer expression of faith that welcomes bodies as they are and is informed by experiences of joy and pleasure more than ascetic resistance. I pray that these young people might catch a glimpse of their beauty and wholeness beyond the insistence that their bodies are full of sin and not to be trusted. And, for the record, food is a way to delight in God's goodness, not to withhold and expect some missing blessing.

In some ways, reading a letter from the ancient world is like over-hearing a conversation, but we only overhear a portion of it. What would that conversation at the coffee shop have looked like if I could only hear the young woman's voice? When we read Revelation and other ancient letters in the New Testament, we only have half of the storyline. Entire libraries are filled with scholars and preachers and theologians filling in the other side of the narrative. We'll explore the contents of the letter in the next chapter, but for now it is important to understand that Revelation is a letter written to specific communities with specific concerns, many of which we simply cannot know.

AN APOCALYPSE

Revelation tells us that it is an apocalypse in the very first word, the title: "The revelation of Jesus Christ." The word translated as "revelation" is the Greek word *apokalypsis*. Revelation cues us into the type of literature we'll be reading in the very first words, also inviting the audience into a long list of expectations about what this book will mean and do for them.

I was an English major in college, and the final course for every senior was a seminar that rotated among the faculty. Each professor could choose the genre based on their interests. Students would choose a piece of literature that fit the theme of the course to write a final thesis. The class ahead of me got to write on works that traveled from page to stage, and to screen. That felt like the jackpot, and I was jealous. My class focused on the historical novel, of which I had read exactly zero in all my time as a reader and a student. It certainly didn't help that we began the course by reading *War and Peace,* which sits (largely unread) on my bookshelf to this day. I didn't feel a pull or excitement from any of the books we read in the seminar, and it took me forever to find a book to focus on. I'd make it halfway through one book only to get bored then move onto the next. Finally, on a whim, I bought a graphic novel more as a diversion to read over spring break.

Watchmen was my jam from the beginning. Disenchanted superheroes, an alternative history where Richard Nixon stays president throughout the Cold War, repressed memories, fringe religious groups, and squid raining from the sky. It was bizarre and beautiful and hopeful and challenging and had all sorts of strange religious themes that I couldn't wait to write about. It was the first (of many) apocalyptic texts that I've fallen in love with. If you get a chance, buy the graphic novel. If you want an adventurous interpretation of it, watch the HBO series from 2019. You won't be disappointed.

On one hand, apocalyptic literature may seem like the most challenging genre of the Bible. It has strange images, often uses poetic discourse that is inaccessible to many of us, and contains violence and sexually explicit imagery. It reaches for the heavens, dives down into the depths, and rarely comes up for air. Apocalyptic literature in the Bible drops references that we lose, assumes knowledge of all the rest of Scripture, makes historical connections and sketches out future visions, all of which are ancient history for us. It's like walking into a world with references that make no sense whatsoever. Preachers often avoid apocalyptic texts because they make people feel uncomfortable. They confront us with harsh words at times, visions we don't understand, and a tone that might not match the soundtrack of poppy Jesus-is-my-boyfriend praise music. But reading the whole of the Bible makes apocalyptic literature unavoidable. Jesus preaches in apocalyptic parables. Paul writes apocalyptic texts in his letters. Prophets like Daniel and Ezekiel use the apocalyptic framework throughout long visions and speeches. And Revelation remains the vexing book at the end of the Bible. Apocalyptic literature may feel foreign to many of us because we have not practiced reading these pages of Scripture.

And yet, in an age of world-building, where comic book characters come back for a new adventure every other month, where fantasy novels are cast in multi-million-dollar, decades-long miniseries, apocalyptic literature is making a comeback of sorts. Take a minute and think about various run-ins with apocalyptic literature. I've already mentioned the disaster story, like *Armageddon* or *Deep Impact* from my adolescence. Next, we have the post-apocalyptic thriller. Some have zombies, some are eco-related, others send us into space. In recent memory, they include *The Walking Dead*, *The Last of Us*, *Mad Max*, and one of my favorites, Octavia Butler's *The Parable of the Sower*. For many of us pandemic fiction gets a little too close to home these days. In *Contagion* Matt Damon is a suburban Minnesota dad (too close to home for me!) whose spouse is patient zero for a virus that mutates from bats and escapes a lab halfway around the world. In a matter of weeks, the world shuts down, millions die, and conspiracy theories are rampant. Perhaps the next too-close-to-home segment of apocalyptic literature and film is the AI takeover. We don't need to watch *Terminator*, *The Matrix*, or *Wall-E* to see the existential threat that artificial intelligence could create. After the release of GPT-4 in the spring of 2023, leaders in academia, technology, and government starkly framed the dangers posed by recent growth in AI: "Mitigating the risk of extinction from AI should be a global priority alongside other societal-scale risks such as pandemics and nuclear war."[20] Apocalyptic fiction sketches the future in terms that feel like they could be here tomorrow.

I could tease out differences in each of these sub-genres, but that is an entire library of studies. We have a language to understand apocalyptic literature in the Bible simply by looking at the popular culture all around us. Apocalyptic literature wakes us up to the consequences that we don't want to face. It suspends our disbelief with zombies, robots, alien invasions, or the threat of environmental catastrophe, but only because we know how close we might be to the consequences of such actions. When we walk into the latest apocalyptic thriller in the theater or re-read *The Hunger Games*, we know what to expect. We'll be frightened, surprised, and eventually a few heroes will solve the problem and save the day. Additionally, what we read is largely influenced by our vantage point. If we are the creators of the killer robot artificial intelligences, there is a warning and a caution. If we are the sector that is displaced by the new advances in technology, we might receive hope that the technology will meet its own ends.

Apocalyptic literature in the Bible would have been met with very similar reviews in the ancient world. People knew what to expect from these strange stories. They could anticipate the jump scares and would understand many of the references being made. Revelation is not the only piece of literature in the Bible that touches on apocalyptic ideas. Noah was asked to bring two of every living creature into a giant ark because God was going to destroy the earth. This isn't a book about Noah, but giants and angels and a naked, drunken encounter of our hero are the lesser-known beats of this Sunday

---

20 Kevin Roose, "AI Poses 'Risk of Extinction,' Industry Leaders Warn," *New York Times*, May 30, 2023, https://www.nytimes.com/2023/05/30/technology/ai-threat-warning.html

school story.[21] The story shows up on the cover of children's Bibles, on baby blankets and mobiles floating over cribs. What a cheery tale to tell our children! The story of Noah isn't an example of apocalyptic literature even though it leaves us with many strange, unanswered, and under-interpreted curves. Apocalyptic literature hadn't been invented yet when Genesis was written. Like the disaster movies that all cropped up in the early 2000s, apocalyptic literature is a development in the later texts we have in the Bible. Much of the prophetic book of Daniel is apocalyptic and large sections of Jeremiah and Ezekiel draw from the apocalyptic tradition. Revelation uses Daniel as source material, shaping images of the beasts from specific visions in the text, connecting Rome's occupation with Daniel's references to Babylon and its destruction of the temple. The Gospels too draw from the apocalyptic tradition in a few of Jesus's teachings and the witness of John the Baptist. Apocalyptic literature is a minor thread in the Scriptures. It isn't on every page, but its voice still preaches with unrestrained acts of imagination.

Because ancient people would understand the contours of this genre of narrative, they would also understand that apocalypse isn't really about the end of the world at all. Buried the lede, didn't I? The Greek word *apokalypsis* means unveiling. Some might take this to mean that if we can unveil the codes and secrets from these strange narratives, we might uncover secret knowledge of sorts. But we've been through this. Revelation is not a code to be cracked, and it's not a blueprint for the end of the world. Revelation is an unveiling, a revealing of Jesus Christ. It is not about the end of the world. Rather, Revelation is a startling vision of the world as it is.

When my eldest daughter was about two, I would often bring her to childcare in our church building before going into my office. Early mornings meant I could leave the office a little earlier in the afternoon to savor the last moments of daylight on cold winter days. One morning, I parked in our usual spot and immediately pulled

---

21 Darren Aronofsky's 2014 film *Noah* stars Russel Crowe and explores some of the stranger contours of this story.

out my phone, checked my email, and was consumed by the to-do list that awaited me. From the back seat I heard a mumble, a stirring, "Daddy . . ." but I kept focused on the tasks at hand, the email that needed a response and the worries of the moment. A bit louder, her little voice insisted, "Daddy! . . ." I couldn't be roused. I'm sure I mumbled something like, "We'll go inside in just one more minute." But she was adamant the third time, and I actually heard her, "Daddy, deer!"

I looked up from my phone, largely annoyed by her persistence. Sitting right in front of us, just three steps away, was a deer, grazing gently on the grass. Tears streamed down my face, not because of the beauty of the scene, though the fog was rising slowly off the prairie grass and the sun was warming the horizon with pink and purple hues. I wasn't crying because of the peaceful presence of another creature that would be startled in just a moment to leap back into the bushes. I was weeping because the veil between the world that I was focused on and the world that my daughter encountered was suddenly lifted. Children have power to do this to us, to somehow give us perspective on the world, transfixed in their vantage by the magic of an ordinary moment. My only response besides the tears welling inside me was to affirm what she saw, "Yes, honey, a deer! Look at that!"

Like Samuel calling for Eli, the priest in the temple, I completely ignored the holiness of the moment in front of me.[22] I lost the mystery and magic of the scene that unfolded before my daughter's very eyes. How many moments have I missed that she has invited me into? How many opportunities have I lost to dance and sing and delight? Apocalypses can be massive in scale, or they can be completely mundane. But isn't this true of the (lower case) revelation of God? The stories of Scripture, and Revelation in particular, attest to the pyrotechnics of the creator of the universe, forming sea and heaven, scattering stars and speaking light. But these ancient texts also call us into the astoundingly ordinary ways God works in our lives, calling our

---

22 1 Samuel 3:1–18

attention toward the world around us and toward one another. What would it look like to name the *revelations* that God is working in your life? Perhaps you will pause (or gasp or delight or wonder) at ordinary interactions with people in the grocery store, children playing in your neighborhood, the sparkling zest of an orange that fills the entire room with fresh, acidic beauty. We'll study God's pyrotechnics together, "the wondrous deeds of the Lord," but I invite you to dwell in the ordinary ways that God is still speaking to us, still revealing mundane moments as interactions with our creator.

3

Churches—Then and Now

In Revelation 21:9–22, we begin a tour of the final verses of Scripture, reading the end of Revelation first and visiting the New City that God inhabits, where worship is embodied by all and the gates are never shut. Then, in Revelation 2–3, we read seven letters that John writes to seven real churches, wondering how they speak to the challenges churches face today. Using the creation poem at the beginning of Genesis 1:1–2:4 as a key, we start to understand the way that the number seven influences all of God's work in Revelation and in our lives.

VACANT CATHEDRALS

I had the first appointment for my driver's license the day I turned sixteen. Driving a car has been freedom to me since that moment. If I'm stuck, I get in the car and go nowhere, often meandering my way into a next step. I like to explore city neighborhoods I've never been in, drive through small towns, and explore farming communities. On a recent trip to visit my spouse's family, I decided to avoid the traffic on the interstate and let the GPS guide me. Towns in Minnesota without post offices or libraries and with populations that could fit in a classroom. Without backseat resistance from my kids, I stopped a few times to admire various church buildings—the tallest structures for miles. Billowing brick buildings with stone carvings of saints and apostles. Belltowers that ring for miles. Steeples stretching skyward. I can hear the hymns even when the doors are locked—weddings and funerals and baptisms, moments of community coming together. But the buildings seem out of place. I understand what they stand for and can imagine the people who gathered to build them. Standing empty however, the vacant cathedrals are haunted by memories that are gone, by a way of life that seems no longer accessible.

Beautiful buildings are an innovation that comes much later in the story of those who followed Jesus. Perhaps your imagination, like mine, immediately conjures one of these skyward structures when you hear the word *church*. But when John writes letters to seven *churches*, he is writing to an entirely different context. John's original audience likely didn't imagine a building at all when they heard the word used throughout the second chapter of Revelation—*ekklesia*, which is likely translated as *church* in your Bible. Part of Revelation is a letter written to seven real communities living in what is now modern-day Turkey. On the pages of your Bible, the second and third chapters stand out like short snippets, each explicitly repetitive, like a paradiddle drum roll before the brass enters with fanfare and holy-holy-holies in Chapter Four.

Several hundred years before the Roman Emperor Constantine converted to Christianity and began constructing massive cathedrals, the seven churches were experiencing the wrath of an entirely different Roman emperor—Nero. We'll talk more about him in Chapter Five, but he is a villain's villain. What our Bibles call *churches* were small communities of people, knit together by a common purpose, wondering about how to define themselves amid a culture that operated by different values. Instead of domed cathedrals, they gathered in homes around a shared meal and worship of the one who was raised. These communities relied on one another for basic needs, shared resources, and were facing very real persecution.

Contemporary *white* Evangelicalism has arrived at a very peculiar definition of this word, *persecution*. Many white Evangelical sermons, churches, and political movements adopt an embattled posture, seeing themselves persecuted by American culture. In one petition, they may pray for an end to the persecution of Christian minorities in China or North Korea. In the next phrase, they may invoke Christian contemporary music lyrics and ask the congregation to help "win this nation back" by combatting the declining morals of our shared community.

When I was about seven, I remember following people in our local congregation down the streets of our city in northern California, holding my first picket sign. I can't remember specifically what it said, but I knew that we were protesting against a world that was "killing babies." In my small parochial school, I remember hearing from teachers that the Ten Commandments were shared American values and should be posted publicly, set in stone at courthouses and post offices for all to see. I remember being taught about the Scopes Monkey Trials, where America started to lose its way in understanding the importance of the creator in our lives. During the first week of high school, I donned my daddy's politics, NRA belt buckle peaking over my Wrangler jeans. I could continue through a setlist of viewpoints that entangle the broader Evangelical movement with conservative politics. People who grew up in similar circles have their own stories to share. My experiences of Evangelical culture are not a universal rule. There indeed are many Evangelical people and even Evangelical churches that embody very different political commitments. Much of my experience is specific to white Evangelicalism and stands in fairly stark contrast to Evangelical circles rooted in the Black church, where politics are intertwined with spirituality in vibrant and contrasting ways to the tradition I grew up in.

But the fact remains that a posture of persecution—pervasive, noisy, powerful—motivates all sorts of expressions of a political and cultural Christian mechanism in the United States. Rather than vacant cathedrals in tucked-away prairie towns, this mechanism is well-funded, media savvy, and reveals itself in all aspects of our common life together. By gathering people around the defensive position, trying to claw back a "once Christian" nation, this mechanism has delivered votes, produced culture, and formed an entire ecosystem and economy of belonging for millions.[1]

Political movements are of course written on newspaper pages and television specials, but they are also written on the bodies and stories of millions of people, myself included. I remember listening to *Adventures in Odyssey* on cassette tape in a minivan. Aired in the time of television, this radio drama embodied the embattlement of a culture under attack. With Saturday morning cartoons, consistent advertising, and all of the threats of the dominant culture run amok, Whit's End was a place where family values held sway, where morality was modeled, and where there was always a happy ending. It was also produced by Focus on the Family, a fundamentalist Evangelical media organization that has consistently lobbied against LGBTQ+ rights, encouraged and advertised conversion therapy,[2] and enforced reactionary gender roles. Tucked neatly between lessons on loving your neighbor were clear political instructions against abortion and homosexuality, and a solid dose of fear.

I can recall one episode in particular called "Castles & Cauldrons," where two kids start playing a fantasy role-playing game that sounds suspiciously (as the title indicates) like Dungeons & Dragons. The two kids get caught up in the game and eventually fall into practicing spells, incantations, and nearly summoning Satan. I can vividly

---

1 Kristin Kobes Du Mez has written extensively about this movement over the past century, offering a revisionist history of sorts regarding the ways that Evangelical culture has reshaped our politics from the ground up, corrupting a faith and fracturing a nation: *Jesus and John Wayne: How White Evangelicals Corrupted a Faith and Fractured a Nation.*

2 A more destructive force in the Evangelical movement, conversion therapy takes the so called "pray the gay away" stance of many white Evangelical churches and wraps it in a pseudo-psychological treatment program. Participation in such "therapies" leads to increased risk of suicide among LGBTQ+ youth. Jamie DuCharme, "Conversion Therapy Is Still Happening in Almost Every U.S. State," *Time*, December 12, 2023, https://time.com/6344824/how-common-is-conversion-therapy-unitedstates

remember nightmares from these cassettes and cautious talks when I was invited to play a role-playing game while backpacking on a Boy Scouts trip. The message was clear—stay vigilant because the world is full of untold dangers that will pull you away from God's goodness. The next time I played D&D was when I was in my mid-thirties. I still can't bring myself to really enjoy it.

Revelation has an overlapping concern with holding firm to the good news, though its visions aren't nearly as frightening as Whit's End. In each of the seven notes written to these seven communities, Revelation offers promises to those who conquer, warnings against false teaching, praise for those who hold firm to the truth, and even a "synagogue of satan." Not exactly bedtime story material, but I once turned a strange section of Revelation into a wild Christmas sermon. The Evangelical insistence on defending an embattled moral position falls flat because it is guarding a powerful definition of American identity—white, upper-middle class, male, cisgender, and heterosexual. Revelation is not a text written to the powerful, who lived in Rome at the time. It is written to those who are being trampled by an oppressive regime with consistent pressure to measure belonging in ways that go against the grain of a newfound faith in Jesus.

CITY LIGHTS (FROM END TO BEGINNING)

There are two reasons that disqualify me from being a true Californian (though my family has lived there for four generations): (1) I don't really like avocados and (2) I've never much cared for the ocean. Growing up, the ocean was too wild, too powerful, too unpredictable (and too cold). When I was young, we always received a lecture before we got close. Remember, the ocean will sneak up on you, so never turn your back on it. The jellyfish sting, so walk around them. Did you hear there have been shark attacks here? Be careful around the tidal pools so you aren't stranded as the tide is coming in again. If all the water rushes back to the ocean quickly, it might be a tidal wave, so run and run fast. And of course, beware of the undertow. If you get caught in one, don't swim straight back, just angle yourself toward the land and swim slow and steady. As a kid, the ocean was just too full of concerns.

Resisting my childhood fear of the ocean, I now use the image of an undercurrent to capture the side of Revelation that you can't quite see on the surface but is tugging nonetheless with lunar gravity. Like a rip tide that slowly draws you out to sea, this pulse is everywhere if you start to notice it. But instead of being drawn inexorably out to sea, we're being drawn into a promise of God. In order to highlight this subtext, we need to actually flip to the very end of Revelation before we begin.

One of my mentors always reads the end of the book first. When she first shared this with me, I was dumbfounded. I think I even did an old-fashioned spit-take with my coffee cup. I love the adventure, the journey, the sense of discovery with any new story, whether on a screen or a page. I never want to read spoilers to movies or novels because it will *spoil* all of the surprise! Revelation is a bit different. It's easy to get stuck in some of the battles, get lost in the calculations, swim into a diversion that ends up dragging us out to sea (wait; I'm mixing my metaphors!). So I make an important exception to my rule for Revelation. We have to know where we are going in order to feel the undercurrent, the minor key pulse of the text.

The final two chapters of Revelation turn from battles and plagues and monsters toward three brilliant visions of God's love—a new creation, a new Jerusalem, and a new garden. Over the next three chapters, we will read the end of Revelation to see the new beginning that God is creating through this vision. I want to start first with the new Jerusalem, or as my friend Tyler Sit calls it, a New City. When Pastor Sit planted New City Church in Minneapolis, the compelling vision that guided their proclamation was Revelation 21, a vision of all of God's goodness centering on a city. But don't take my word for it. Here's what their "about us" says on the website: "New City got its name from Revelation 21, which describes a heaven where God lives in a 'new city' where all tribes are welcomed in, where there is no more violence, and where the whole earth is renewed. Our community reflects this vision, as we have members with all kinds of racial/ethnic identities, socioeconomic statuses, gender and sexual identities, intellectual and physical abilities, immigration statuses, and religious beliefs."[3] For those of us who continue to hear stories of the church's decline, Tyler and New City Church sing a brand-new song, gathering an almost entirely millennial and Generation Z crowd to learn about Jesus and serve the city of Minneapolis. Tyler jokes that his parents drastically increase the average age of New City members when they come to church. One of the hidden gems of the pandemic season is that I could sneak in on New City worship services virtually when I was leading my own community just a few miles away.

I love New City Church because I have always loved the energy and constant evolution of cities. I have pushed against the narratives of deficit that sometimes plague suburban imaginations by bringing young people into Minneapolis to see its beauty, delight in its contours, and celebrate its gifts, rather than simply "serve" its problems. Growing up, "the city" was San Francisco, a seven-square-mile peninsula straddling ocean and bay that I would take any excuse to visit. Before I could make trips of my own, my fourth-grade class spent the night on a living museum—a schooner built in 1895 that welcomes school children for overnight experiences of life on a sailing vessel. I'm sure my love for this city began in the early morning hours on galley crew, climbing to the top of the ship and watching the sun rise over the city, the Ghirardelli sign flickering out as the sky was painted with pastels. In high school we'd take the ferry, hop on Bay Area Rapid Transit (BART), or get in my '74 Volkswagen 181 to explore the namesake of the region and our temple to northern California culture. It took an hour or more to get there, which meant it wasn't an everyday trip. It felt special, set apart, like a pilgrimage of sorts. Cannoli in North Beach and tea in Golden Gate Park. Dim sum in Chinatown and hot fudge in Ghirardelli Square. I can still spend hours in City Lights Bookstore, pulling titles from bookshelves, soaking in the stories of Lawrence Ferlinghetti, Allen Ginsberg, and Jack Kerouac.

---

3 https://grownewcity.church/about-us

The glorious vision at the end of Revelation insists that God's goodness resides in the midst of the city. One of the seven angels who held seven bowls of plagues (there's your number seven again!) calls John forward: "Come, I will show you the bride, the wife of the Lamb."[4] The beloved of Christ is a gleaming city, the New Jerusalem. John looks down on the city from a high mountain as it descends from heaven to reside among mortals. The city is described in intimate detail, sets of twelve repeating throughout (angels, gates, and foundations), representing the twelve tribes of Israel and the twelve disciples. Measurements are provided, recalling descriptions of the temple and the tabernacle, enumerated in excruciating detail in Leviticus. The measurements have symbolic significance. Multiples of twelve (12,000 stadia, 144,000 cubits) recall the twelve tribes of Israel but also incorporate all the nations of earth. If you were to sketch this image on graph paper, it would be among the largest cities on earth. The angel measures the contours of the city before John: "The city has four equal sides, its length the same as its width, and he measured the city with his rod, twelve thousand stadia; its length and width and height are equal."[5] Measured at 12,000 stadia, the length, width, and height are roughly 1,380 miles each. Los Angeles is 745 square miles, and its tallest building is 1,100 feet (0.2 miles). Tokyo is the largest city in the world by population with a United Nations estimate of 37.5 million people living in it. Tokyo is 1,361 square miles, still smaller than the New Jerusalem. The tallest building in Tokyo is 2,080 feet (0.3 miles) and nowhere near the height of this city. Made famous by Tom Cruise's stunt in *Mission Impossible 3* as he climbed it with suction cups, the tallest building in the world is the Burj Kalifa in Dubai. It stretches 2,717 feet high, more than half a mile into the sky. It would take more than 2,600 Burj Kalifas to stretch to the height of the New Jerusalem. While John may be exaggerating to make a point (hyperbole for any other English majors reading), describing a city that is far

---

4 Revelation 21:9
5 Revelation 21:16

larger than any imaginable on the planet, the measurements of the city show us the expanse of God's love for all of creation. God is not building a small town where only a few are welcome. God doesn't select only the moral best or few most faithful to inherit this city. God is a grand architect for a glorious city where "People will bring into it the glory and the honor of the nations."[6] Precious materials like jasper and gold appear on every corner, revealing "the glory of God and a radiance like a fine jewel."[7] The streets glisten with the finest material of the earth, the rich diversity of God's creation, to welcome people into this glorious new city.

But the most profound verse of this vision is still to come: "I saw no temple in the city, for its temple is the Lord God the Almighty and the Lamb."[8] In the ancient Jewish world (John's world), the temple was the center of economic, social, and religious life. It was where God resided, in the Holy of Holies, where the high priest would walk but once a year to whisper the name of God. Some traditions have even said that they would tie a rope around the priest's ankle, so they could drag him out if he was impure and struck down by God's holiness. I'll confess, I'm glad these are not part of my priestly duties.

The absence of a temple in Revelation is both a political challenge and a theological promise. It is likely that Revelation was written after the siege of Jerusalem, the final and decisive battle in the first Jewish–Roman war, where the temple was destroyed by the Romans. A bit of history is a great help in reading Revelation, so bear with me if you didn't study Latin in college or haven't made friends with Josephus or Pliny the Elder (or if the only reason you know the latter is the fabulous beer brewed in Santa Rosa, California).

Our best guess is that Jesus lived right around the hinge when we start counting forward from backward. We don't know exact years but have some well-educated guesses (and libraries arguing over the details). I was taught "BC" for "Before Christ" and "AD" for "Anno

---

6 Revelation 21:26
7 Revelation 21:11
8 Revelation 21:22

Domini," or year of our Lord. Many folks today use BCE (before common era) and CE (common era). Historians estimate that Jesus was crucified (a Roman punishment reserved only for slaves, pirates, and enemies of the state) between 30 and 33 CE. The New Testament was largely written well after Jesus lived and taught. The earliest texts are the letters from Paul, written between 48 and 62 CE. The gospels come next—Mark around 66–70 CE, Matthew and Luke around 80–85 CE, and John much later, around 90–110 CE. Revelation was written somewhere around 95 CE, when most of the people who walked alongside Jesus had died. This might rearrange a lot of mental furniture if you've grown up in Evangelical circles, including exposure to deep Bible studies like Bible Study Fellowship. Many of these programs follow tradition rather than scholarship, common sense, or curiosity. They connect all of the books in the New Testament with people who walked alongside Jesus and witnessed his miracles and teachings directly. The scholarly consensus of a much later context provides a way to understand the meaning of Revelation's vision of a new Jerusalem that would make little sense if it were written by someone who walked alongside Jesus in Nazareth.

Rome was the superpower of the world when Jesus was alive and when the New Testament was written. The world was living under the Pax Romana, an extended season of peace through brutal imperial authority and power. As the empire expanded, Roman rulers would bring economics and religious practices of their own, while allowing space for local flavor. Rome was fairly tolerant of local religious groups. It was a part of their business plan for the empire. If locals could worship their own regional deities, they were less likely to rise up and revolt, costing the empire money and men. While this may have worked in other parts of the world, Jerusalem was a problem.

The Jewish religion was and is monotheistic, believing in one God. The Hebrew Bible is full of reminders that "I am the Lord your God and you shall have no other gods before me."[9] But Roman citizens brought Roman customs, Roman culture, and Roman gods. Our

---

9 For example, from the Ten Commandments in Exodus 20:1–17.

planets are named after them: Mars, the god of war; Venus, the goddess of desire, sex, and fertility; Neptune, the god of the sea, and so on. Further, the emperor of Rome was deified, considered part of the pantheon, revered, and worshipped. A common phrase in the ancient world was *Kaiser kurios*, or Caesar is Lord. More than dissonant to Jews whose central affirmation is the *shema* ("Hear Israel, the Lord is our God. The Lord is one")[10], this proclamation also went against some of the earliest confessions of the followers of Christ—Jesus is Lord. The religious friction specific to Jerusalem emboldened and gave credibility to movements that emerged to overthrow the Roman rule at this economic crossroads to the world. There were three major revolts against Rome, the first of which got going right as the New Testament was being written.

After the first Jewish War, Rome surrounded and besieged Jerusalem, finally destroying the temple, and along with it the center of Jewish identity and the home of God. When John dreams of a *new* Jerusalem after the city had been sacked and the temple destroyed, he is offering an incredibly compelling vision for a people whose entire identity had been questioned in the destruction. Echoing the prophets of the Hebrew Bible, John paints a picture of God's love making its home in the beautiful city of Jerusalem, descending from heaven as a bride to Christ: "See the home of God is among mortals."[11] Rather than tucked away in the Holy of Holies, God is on the city streets, where people from all corners of the world join in worship to the Lamb. God's presence radiates from the bricks on the streets, with gates flung wide open for all people to enjoy.

Maybe you've heard the one about St. Peter. Or, rather, the nine hundred about St. Peter at the pearly gate. The punchline comes from this section of Revelation, where the gates are described: "And the twelve gates are twelve pearls, each of the gates is a single pearl, and the street of the city is pure gold, transparent as glass."[12] But

---

10 Deuteronomy 6:4–9
11 Revelation 21:3
12 Revelation 21:21

Peter isn't defending the gate, interviewing all who enter, ensuring who is in and who is out. Rather, these gates are left wide open: "Its gates will never be shut by day—and there will be no night there."[13] God resides throughout the city, beckoning people to enjoy the new creation that God is making, the beginning of something entirely new. As we read the last few verses of Scripture, we can also learn alongside the *beginning* of creation itself, where God promises to preserve all that was and is and will forever be.

WHOLLY NUMBER SEVEN

One of my favorite holy places is now an abandoned chapel at the seminary I attended in St. Paul, Minnesota, a stark, uber-modern box with a hulking brass sculpture of Jesus on the cross in the center. Seminary students were required to preach our first attempts at sermons from its concrete pulpit that dominated the room. Any time I entered, a hush met me through the heavy double doors. A sacred space with startlingly few windows, the only natural light came through small slits near the altar. illuminating seven hanging lamps over the massive concrete table. I didn't know why there were seven until I fell headlong into the first and last books of the Bible. Perhaps the end is the beginning.

Numbers show up all over the place in Revelation, and it can feel a bit dizzying. Which numbers mean something? How do I make sense of these various numbers? Much has been written and preached and predicted about these numbers using a version of Hebrew math called gematria. Calculations and references to this tradition can send you down lengthy rabbit holes full of fierce predictions of the end of the world. I haven't taken a mathematics class since junior year of high school, so I won't be spinning any visions of dates for the end of the world for us. I will however discuss this tradition a bit more when we get to the number 666 in Chapter Five. As you

---

13 Revelation 21:35

read through Revelation, you need to know that there are some numbers that are significant and others that have no agreed-upon meaning. The uncertain numbers are of course fertile ground for conspiracy and prediction, but for now, we start with a consistent number in Revelation and across Scripture: seven.

If you're reading along in the first two chapters of Revelation, you have already read the number seven all over the place. John mentions that this vision is for the seven churches in Asia but also references seven spirits, seven lampstands, seven stars, and receiving this vision on the seventh day (the Lord's day). In case anyone snoozed through the first chapter of Revelation, Jesus himself decodes the words, "As for the mystery of the seven stars that you saw in my right hand and the seven golden lampstands: the seven stars are the angels of the seven churches, and the seven lampstands are the seven churches."[14] Got it, there are seven messages for seven churches. But why the obsession with seven (which we're not even close to done with, by the way)?

That will involve going back to the first verses of the Bible, a sort of super decoder ring of reading Hebrew Scripture—the creation story. In parochial school I was taught that God created the heavens, the earth, and all that is in them in seven literal twenty-four-hour periods. If you've spent much time at all in fundamentalism or perhaps visited the strange Creation Museum in Kentucky, you understand this essential conviction of Evangelical faith. Whether through seven twenty-four-hour periods or some other gymnastic reading of geology, creationism frequently denies that the earth is billions of years old and always denies any theory of the evolution of species. But there is always a problem with the dinosaurs.[15]

---

14 Revelation 1:20

15 I'm not a scientist, but I think science has a lot of important things to teach us. One of my favorite theologians has written a really helpful book to help make science and faith talk to one another rather than argue all the time. There are many more books like this, but Andy's is a good start: *Exploding Stars, Dead Dinosaurs, and Zombies: Youth Ministry in the Age of Science* (Minneapolis: Fortress Press, 2018).

I could sit here and argue how they are all mistaken. But I've found that arguing with people about these sorts of ideas generally goes nowhere. It is much more interesting to see how creationist approaches to the creation story miss the beautiful and brilliant poetic structure of these first verses of Scripture. I'm not here to convince anyone that the Bible was created in six literal days or to show the proof points of the Big Bang theory or the theory of evolution. Rather, I invite us into a poem at the beginning of the Bible that answers questions about *why* we are here much better than how we got here. Because this book is about Revelation and not Genesis, I'll resist the temptation to go down a rabbit hole and list all of the sevens in the first chapter of the Bible, but suffice it to say they are everywhere.[16] There are obviously seven days in the creation story, but also there are structures of seven words and seven syllables and seven paragraphs that echo throughout the poem. There are also repetitions that happen seven times, a pulsing drumbeat of blessing: "Evening and morning" and "God saw that it was good." The number seven ripples throughout every corner of the Bible. Jesus teaches us to forgive seven-times-seventy times. Hebrew festivals were sets of sevens. The Levitical laws set out a sabbatical year every seven years to let the land lie fallow, rest, and find new life. And the seven-times-seventh year was a year of jubilee where all debts were forgiven, enslaved people were freed, and immigrants were made citizens. And of course, most importantly, the sabbath occurs on the seventh day, when God rested and celebrated all the good that God had done. When God blesses this seventh day, God also "hallows it," makes it holy, or separate. Our Jewish siblings practice keeping the sabbath, intentionally pausing for rest and worship every seventh day. My

---

16 If you want to nerd out on the number seven, check out the podcast from the folks at The Bible Project, an Evangelical organization. I am glad the folks behind all of the videos and podcasts and articles are reaching for a broader way to read the Scriptures. While I sometimes disagree with them, I find a lot of their resources really helpful. You can listen to their hosts riff on seven here: https://bibleproject.com/podcast/significance-7/

stepmom's family are Seventh Day Adventists who attend Sabbath School and practice rest, prayer, and reading Scripture that day.[17]

The number seven throughout Scripture refers to completion, fullness, or wholeness. Creation is not complete without rest. We are not whole without sabbath. In Revelation, the number seven aligns with Jesus's proclamation that he is the alpha and the omega, the first and last letters of the Greek alphabet, the beginning and the end. God ultimately resides in the midst of the city, calling something new into being right from the streets and neighborhoods and parks and lakes. These seven churches, set in heavenly terms, point us to the broader story of what God is doing through these faithful communities. From beginning to end (alpha and omega) and to a new beginning, Jesus is gathering all of creation in love through the witness of these flawed and faithful churches. Pointing to a vision where God resides in the midst of the city, needing no temple because love is on the loose, Revelation encourages contemporary Christians to wrestle with the ways our churches are forming an alternative imagination or simply exemplifying the culture that exists around us.

A TALE OF TWO CHURCHES

Consummate church-rats, my daughters can often be found downing donuts in "daddy's office" in between worship services or after school. Winter gets long in the far north where we live. Usually on the seventh consecutive sub-zero day, we go to church when no one is there, bring scooters or skateboards or remote control cars, and let them run up and down the hallways. They explore rooms and closets and beg to go on the roof or in the "dungeon." (To be clear, our church doesn't actually have a dungeon; it is a storage and air-handling

---

17 This book is not about sabbath. But if it were, I would share more with you from three fabulous books on the topic: Dr. Walter Brueggeman's *Sabbath as Resistance: Saying No to the Culture of Now*, Rabbi Abraham Joshua Heschel's *The Sabbath*, and Nathan Stuckey's *Wrestling with Rest: Inviting Youth to Discover the Gift of Sabbath*.

room with untold treasures and surprises that we strangely refer to as the dungeon.) Our kids find endless entertainment in the random things they can find at church—in the lost-and-found, youth room, or kitchen. I often have a package of sticky notes on my desk, which, aside from the overstuffed leather chair, is probably my daughters' favorite feature of my office. Usually hustling to get out the door on any given Sunday, I will return Monday morning to find little orange and blue squares littering every corner of my window and computer monitor, square Astrobright canvases with sparkly pictures of pandas, goofy words like "poop-dad," and the rare reminder that they love me.

Revelation begins with a series of notes, written to "the seven churches in Asia." For the globally aware, we are looking at Asia *Minor*, which is contemporary Turkey, a crossroads of global trade and an important economic hub for the Roman Empire. In just a few short verses, these letters look a bit like sticky notes in your open Bible. They may have headlines that say, "The message to . . ." seven real cities. Each of these brief addresses speak to a real church, with specific instructions that are wrapped in rich poetry.

Rather than walking through all seven, I'll tell a tale of two churches, selecting two of the sticky notes that slice both ways. As the Scriptures say about themselves, "the word of God is living and active and sharper than any two-edged sword, piercing until it divides soul from spirit, joints from marrow."[18] I have spent a lot of time picking on the Evangelical mechanism that formed me, but Revelation also has a strong critique for the mainline moderate or progressive Protestant churches that I serve now. Ephesus and Laodicea, the first and last churches in this sequence of sticky notes, serve as perfect foils for one another. I'll also make comparisons to two real churches that I have come into contact with. But, to avoid hurt feelings, I've made them anonymous. These little notes are stunning analogues to real churches in our midst. Read all seven and wonder with me

---

18 Hebrews 4:12

what churches in your community might need to hear each word of Revelation.

As John writes short notes to seven different churches, he is also helping us see a vision of Jesus through each of these stories, shining the character of Christ through seven different lenses. When we encounter Jesus in Revelation, he looks and sounds very different from the Jesus of the gospels. He isn't teaching in parables, turning over tables in the temple, healing sick people, or feeding a crowd with a few loaves and fish. The images of Jesus from Revelation look a whole lot more like comic books than stories from Sunday school. But that doesn't mean they are entirely unfamiliar. I'll spend a bit of time with the affirmations and challenges John offers to each of these communities, then invite us to laugh together about how these churches might still show up in our contemporary imagination.

Ephesus

To the angel of the church in Ephesus write: These are the words of him who holds the seven stars in his right hand, who walks among the seven golden lampstands: I know your works, your toil and your endurance. I know that you cannot tolerate evildoers; you have tested those who claim to be apostles but are not and have found them to be false. I also know that you are enduring and bearing up for the sake of my name and that you have not grown weary. But I have this against you, that you have abandoned the love you had at first. Remember, then, from where you have fallen; repent and do the works you did at first. If not, I will come to you and remove your lampstand from its place, unless you repent. Yet this is to your credit: you hate the works of the Nicolaitans, which I also hate. Let anyone who has an ear listen to what the Spirit is saying to the churches. To everyone who conquers, I will give permission to eat from the tree of life that is in the paradise of God.[19]

---

19 Revelation 2:1–7

Visions of Jesus

"These are the words of him who holds the seven stars in his right hand, who walks among the seven golden lampstands." We've already heard Jesus say what these seven golden lampstands are—the seven churches. Jesus is walking among the seven churches, actively proclaiming, actively moving, physically present in the rituals of worship and meal. Jesus is present in this church, though there is a clear threat. If these people do not return to the ways of love, Jesus will remove the lamp from their assembly. Losing the way of love is losing the presence of the living Christ. This vision of Jesus also holds the seven stars. Recalling the stars (as signs) from Genesis 1, Christ holds creation in the palm of his hand, the power to preserve the architecture of the heavens and the earth with his pulse. Our first sticky note has a sketch of Jesus who holds creation in his palm and walks among the churches who worship him, present in their persecution and their proclamation.

Affirmations

Jesus is actively practicing what my spouse calls the Oreo method of communicating "feedback"—offer some affirmations on either end of what might be a criticism, or area for improvement. The Ephesian church is known for its works—for enduring persecution, rooting out false teachers, holding firm to the name of Jesus, and not giving up. This community would be pretty good at the comment section of every YouTube video, pointing out the mistakes of each preacher and bringing everyone else down in the process. They know what the right teaching is and are going to kick any people who don't fit the doctrine to the curb.

The New Testament is full of a back-and-forth between a few different voices who are trying to discredit the others. We don't have access to many texts that lost the arguments, but instead have the thread that was passed on to the next generation. It is important to note that there was no final draft of what it means to be a

Christian while the New Testament was being written. Instead, we have a variety of voices vying for perspective, jockeying for authority, borrowing names from one another, and sometimes openly dissing their opponents. About three hundred years later, the ecumenical councils met to more formally discern what Christian faith might look like. At these giant committee hearings, the church debated the finer points of theology (like did God share the same *ousia* with Jesus?).[20] But the honest truth is that there has never been a final draft of Christian faith. Rather, the story of Christianity is a story of reckoning, wrestling, discerning, disagreeing, and ultimately evolving. Paul had a piece; the gospel writers too; John his own. But the early church mothers and fathers shaped how we read these Scriptures and began pointing to texts that held more authority. Split after split, splinter after splinter, the family tree continued to diversify in belief and in practice, through the Great Schism of 1094 between Roman Catholic and Eastern Orthodox and the Reformation sparked in 1517 by Martin Luther's ninety-five theses. The story continues today in denominational disagreements, ecumenical conversations, and interfaith dialogue. To those of us who have moved from one tradition to another only to find that it has faults of its own, this is truly good news. Jesus is present among the churches, holding creation in the palm of his hand, receiving the rich diversity of human worship, affirming what works, correcting what is harmful.

Two times, Revelation mentions false teachers (once in the note to the Ephesians and the second time in the note to Thyatira) who are leading other Christians astray with false teachings. They are called the Nicolaitans, and it is likely that they taught an amalgamation of local cultural practices alongside Christian rites. So one day you could worship with other Christians, and the next you could eat the

---

20 I won't be spending a bunch of time on the complicated history of the canon and the formation of Christian doctrine, but if you are curious, take a look at John Philip Jenkins's book, *Jesus Wars: How Four Patriarchs, Three Queens, and Two Emperors Decided What Christians Would Believe for the Next 1,500 Years.*

food offered up to the local Roman deity—Jupiter, Aphrodite, or the emperor himself. They also may have practiced temple prostitution, a commonly held Roman practice that was forbidden in Jewish worship. We gather much of this intel from the third sticky note written to the church in Thyatira. Revelation insists that Christians stand apart from the Roman culture that is all around. It draws a line of participation in the church that may feel very foreign to many of us who grew up with freedom of religion and the veritable marketplace of religious practices in the United States. When the letter asks the church to stand firm, it is asking them to stand apart, separate, and distinct from the local culture.

Challenges

Perhaps the most touching and applicable of all the challenges in these sticky notes, the Ephesians are criticized for having "abandoned the love you had at first." Paul might call them noisy gongs or clanging symbols,[21] prophets and priests who have abandoned love in favor of righteous works. We know these folks—people who hold doctrine like a shield while ignoring people who are left out, cast aside, and actively hurt by checklists of orthodoxy. This church has mixed up its messaging and its purpose, quickly hating the false teachers and completely abandoning love. The reckoning that I felt early on in my time of deconstruction was ultimately coming to terms with a faith that I believed had lost its ability to love. I read about a Jesus who ate with sinners and scoffed at religious authorities and thought the church I grew up in looked more like a club for religious insiders than a community that emulated the company that Jesus kept. I saw lists of vices a mile long, insistence on purity, and chasing away folks who fell outside the norms set by the community rather than a community flowing out of the love experienced in Jesus's arms.

---

21 1 Corinthians 13:1

Churches Today

Whenever the topic of "homosexuality" came up in youth group (using the most fabulous air-quotes because nobody I know calls themself a "homosexual"; rather it is used by folks who want to highlight who and how they love in the sheets over who they are in the world), someone would always recite the common phrase, "Love the sinner. Hate the sin." Perhaps your in-laws and the cousin who just found Jesus at the hipster megachurch still return to it. For some churchy insiders, it may seem right. We resist the sin, but we love with all our being the sinner, pray for their redemption, and hope that they can overcome their pension for sinfulness with a little help from Jesus. But like many little cultural truisms, it quickly falls apart.

For all of my growing up years, I knew my two uncles who lived together. They always bought the coolest Christmas presents and seemed to live lives that exceeded my imagination for what was possible, jet setting the globe for business, attending lavish parties, and lots of water skiing. I remember when I started to figure out that they weren't just roommates living in Chicago, that they loved each other and were a couple. I also remember clearly the conversation that I had in the car with my mom. "We love your uncle, but we don't support 'his lifestyle.'" I didn't quite even know what that meant. Was it the fancy cars and flamboyant clothing? Or maybe it was the trips or their giant bird?

My family has been on a journey of welcome and acceptance and eventually affirmation. At times I fought, tooth and nail, against my family's apathetic acceptance of Evangelical dogma that gay people are full of sin. When I was in college, California was voting on Proposition 8, a coordinated campaign to outlaw gay marriage through a ballot initiative. I had protested the bill from Minnesota as the entire country watched the most "progressive" state in the nation outlaw same-sex marriage. Returning home for the holidays, I remember yelling at my elders over a Christmas meal about voting for the bill. Full of conviction, I wanted to teach them. It left all of us hurting and did very little good. But lately, I've been amazed that the far less audacious, slow, careful conversations have actually changed hearts and minds. My mom has started reading books that have completely shifted her perspective. She raises her concerns to family friends and Bible study groups, trying to broaden people's perspective of who is welcome at Jesus's table of love. I think influenced by conversations we've had, she risks speaking up to friends who think differently, connecting with her friends' adult children who have already moved beyond "this issue." It means the world to me.

But it also hurts. When my grandfather died, I sat between my grandmother and my uncle at the funeral, the namesake of my papa. I know that my grandfather never had a change of heart. I know that even at the end of his life, he was praying that his son might change his mind or return to a different "lifestyle." The tears that we shed together at the funeral were about more than missing this man who found his emotions through Promise Keepers, introduced me to Revelation through *Left Behind*, and paid me a quarter for every toilet in the church that we cleaned together. We cried about the way that this church had shut humanity out and had left love behind. We cried tears for relationships that might never be fully affirmed, welcomed, accepted, or celebrated in a building that has meant so much to our family. I'm still crying. I'm still healing. And I know so many are too.

I know, I trust, I believe, and I confess that the creator of the universe, the sustainer of all that was and is and is to come, wiped our tears that day. For a book filled with the most fiery visions, fierce battles, and provocative indictments, God leans in with a whisper and a promise: "And God shall wipe all tears from their eyes."[22] God moves toward the pain, brokenness, mourning, and grief of our existence, wiping the tears from our eyes, and pointing us to the wonder that is being created all around.

---

22 Revelation 21:3

Our First Modern-Day Church

After college I led the youth group for a little liberal church on the campus of our giant land-grant university in Minneapolis in a neighborhood lovingly called Dinkytown. It is a delightful little congregation and community that was patient with my doubts, challenges, curiosities, and messy spots and gave me the grace to lead in and through a sticky season of deconstruction. We gathered a "Dream Team" that planned youth activities for professors' kids—spunky, curious, brainy goofballs, who I adored. One year, the team wanted to learn about different kinds of Christians—how they worship, what their buildings look like, and so on. On a crisp October Sunday morning, we took them down the road to a cathedral of a certain focused expression of Evangelical thought across the nation. Our kids didn't know what to make of it. But we had a rich conversation over donuts after the ninety-minute worship service featuring two songs, an hour of sermon, and a lengthy prayer.

I first became aware of this church and its superstar preacher through my friend, Steven, who grew up in the same California congregation. We share memories of skateboarding in the church parking lot, youth group lock-ins, music festivals, and my personal favorite, singing "I'm in the Lord's Army" in the church Christmas pageant while wearing red sweat suits gussied up to look like nutcrackers. Steven had recently started attending a hip new church in Brooklyn where he had moved a few years earlier. His small group was patiently reading through a glut of flashy paperbacks by a so-called "Young, Restless, and Reformed Movement." The preacher at this church down the road was the elder statesman among these authors, the guy that all the up-and-coming theobros[23] would quote

---

23 Trademark Natalia Terfa, with help from Meta Herrick Carlson. A theobro sits on a stool to show you his goatee and forearm tattoo, ripped jeans. He thinks he's progressive because he'll mansplain mansplaining to you. He'll interrupt your experience of being a woman to tell you he knows women and lives with one.

when they needed to look respectful to their elders and wanted to increase their apparent quotient of *substantia grisea*.

The church had a clear understanding of its doctrine, its dogma, and the things in the culture it stood against—to name a few, egalitarianism, "gender politics," radical feminism, elite scholasticism, and many more. The large sanctuary had no artwork but was warm in the morning light. It was also startlingly empty. But folks in the pews looked pretty proud to be there. In the words of Revelation, this church had traded the love at the heart of Christian understanding for insistence on right belief. In their effort to root out heresy or amorality, this church and the movement that followed it led people through gauntlets of purity culture, morality policing, proof of sanctification, and lost love in the process. For a congregation who stated that they desired God's presence, the sanctuary felt cold and heartless. "And if I have prophetic powers and understand all mysteries and all knowledge and if I have all faith so as to remove mountains but do not have love, I am nothing."[24]

Revelation cuts both ways with sharp criticism for churches like this who have abandoned love, but it also lays down the gauntlet for congregations who have different challenges. Like Paul's anger at the Galatians, Revelation does not hold back, but the diversity of the criticism and affirmation invites us to have an honest appraisal of the traditions that have formed each of us, wondering about the gifts and the baggage that come along with living in Christian community.

Laodicea

And to the angel of the church in Laodicea write: The words of the Amen, the faithful and true witness, the origin of God's creation: I know your works; you are neither cold nor hot. I wish that you were either cold or hot. So, because you are lukewarm and neither cold nor hot, I am about to spit you out of my mouth. For you say, "I am rich, I have prospered, and I need

---

24 1 Corinthians 13:2

nothing." You do not realize that you are wretched, pitiable, poor, blind, and naked. Therefore I advise you to buy from me gold refined by fire so that you may be rich, and white robes to clothe yourself and to keep the shame of your nakedness from being seen, and salve to anoint your eyes so that you may see. I reprove and discipline those whom I love. Be earnest, therefore, and repent. Listen! I am standing at the door, knocking; if you hear my voice and open the door, I will come in and eat with you, and you with me. To the one who conquers I will give a place with me on my throne, just as I myself conquered and sat down with my Father on his throne. Let anyone who has an ear listen to what the Spirit is saying to the churches.[25]

Visions of Jesus

Perhaps the most poetic description is the last of these seven sticky notes: "The words of the Amen, the faithful and true witness, the origin of God's creation." Jesus is the omega, yes, but Jesus is also the liturgical affirmation, the blessing and benediction of all that is. When I'm preaching in the churches and pulpits I serve most, Lutherans sometimes poke fun at me when I ask for too many "amens" (they also say them wrong, with a long *ah* rather than an *ay*). In this sticky note, Jesus is described as the amen, which is the final word of a prayer, the affirmation of good news, and the benediction of creation itself.

You might remember that, back to the beginning again, the creation story echoes with a rhythm of repeated words: "and God saw that it was good." The blessing spoken over creation, over plants and trees, stars and seas, tiny creatures and you and me, is a promise that we are created good, in the image of God. Again, rewiring some of the circuits in our theological imagination, the first word spoken over humanity is that we are "indeed very good." It isn't original sin or total depravity but goodness, not a curse of perfection but an affirmation

---

25 Revelation 3:14–22

of enough. God makes human beings good through the ongoing and unfolding action of creation. Our efforts and our accomplishments, our beliefs and our morality, do not determine the word God speaks over humanity. We are created in God's image, reflecting God's goodness in the world. These seven sticky notes echo the creation story all over. Repeating phrases and structures, and recalling ideas from Genesis, our opening vision is almost meant to call the people around the campfire, to hear anew a story that they've heard for generations, when God started creating. The end is the beginning.

Jesus is also the "origin of God's creation." Wow. I love how this verse reverses the alpha and omega to be the amen and the origin. It's the only place in Revelation where there is play and dance in this formula. Everywhere else, Jesus proclaims that he is the alpha and the omega, the beginning and the end. But in this little verse, Jesus is the not-so-final end of the prayer and the very first word of creation. Jesus is the substance that creation flows from, the word spoken into the brooding chaotic waters, the affirmation of our goodness, and the invitation into the ongoing work of creation itself. Already in the third chapter of Revelation, we are seeing cues that this is not about the end of everything but a new kind of beginning, where God's creation is made whole, where the promises of the first verses of Scripture are brought home through the love and mystery of Jesus.

Affirmations

Uff. No cookies around this little sticky note. Laodicea gets only challenge. A few of the churches just receive reprimand. But there is always an invitation into faithfulness. It happens at the end of the section: "Listen! I am standing at the door, knocking; if you hear my voice and open the door, I will come in and eat with you, and you with me." Doors and gates appear everywhere in Revelation. As we've discussed, contemporary imagination keeps the doors shut, with Peter sifting out the worthy from the unworthy, the sinners from the saints. But doors in Revelation are most often standing wide open. The shut door here is from the church. Jesus is waiting outside, knocking and waiting for an invitation, but the door won't open! Jesus wants to dine with this church, to share a meal of love and community, but the people have shut the door, locked him out. The promise remains, though: simply open the door, and Jesus will come in for supper. Throughout all of the great cosmic battles of Revelation, Jesus appears intimately, in ordinary moments, wiping tears and eating at our tables.

Challenges

Contending with Revelation and "The Second Coming," W. B. Yeats said it right: "The best lack all conviction, while the worst / Are full of passionate intensity."[26] Tepid, lukewarm, half-hearted, dull, apathetic, mild. This church doesn't stand for anything. Just like the Ephesians, "I know your works." But rather than expressing pride in the way that Laodicea has stood for faith, Revelation chides them: "you are neither cold nor hot. I wish you were either cold or hot." The church in Laodicea is wealthy and thinks that it needs nothing. If they cannot rely on Jesus, trusting in the gifts that come from faith, the letter warns, "I am about to spit you out." Like the whale that erps Jonah onto the shore, Jesus will spit this flavorless proclamation out, rejecting it completely.

A Second Modern-Day Church

A friend of mine once worked at a church that measures itself by the minute. Packing and stacking people into worship services, preaching for no more than eight minutes, singing the greatest hits of hymns throughout the centuries, and sending people on their way without a morsel of sacrament.

One of the things that drove him a bit bonkers was a discussion about reading the president's Thanksgiving Proclamation as the

---

26 William Butler Yeats, "The Second Coming," *The Collected Poems of W. B. Yeats* (New York: Scribner, 1996).

sermon for their Thanksgiving worship service. I did a spit take over beer, hearing the story. I had no idea the president proclaimed anything on Thanksgiving, let alone something of value to read in place of a sermon in a church service. I've seen the episode of the *West Wing* at least a dozen times, when C. J. Cregg gets stuck with two turkeys to pardon in her office and is forced to pick one. But I've got bones to pick with a congregation that opens its pulpit to voice a proclamation from the president.

This congregation was built to work well for a specific varietal of powerful man, who wants to rub elbows with likeminded and like-positioned individuals in various aspects of life. Like a country club, it can be a place where needs are met and relationships forged. Real estate deals, political campaigns, and philanthropic endeavors are all built in the halls of this cathedral church. But perhaps it, like those gathered in Laodicea, feels more like the halls of a country club than a sanctuary for sinners. Perhaps the folks gathered are lulled into complacency by a faith that is so otherworldly that it ignores the pressing issues of the moment. Perhaps by avoiding politics, it avoids the very heartbeat of the gospel, pulsing hot blood through unhoused and drug addicted and beloved people. Perhaps paintings of former senior leaders solidify a vision for leadership that leaves far too many without a seat at the table. Perhaps the church coffee is flavorless and lukewarm, and the spirit of the place stands for almost nothing.

Or perhaps I'm off my rocker. You decide, and fill in these caricatures with those of your community. If we can't poke a little fun at one another, I think we avoid the calling of this text to stand for things that matter, to draw a line in the sand for the kind of community we will be, and to hear the call of Jesus persistently opening doors to all.

4

Worship from Longfellow to Leipzig

Worship is a guiding rhythm to the Book of Revelation. It is a cycle that each strange vision returns to over and again. You can find these worship cycles in Revelation 4:1–11; 7:1–17; 11:15–19; 15:1–4; 19:1–10; and 21:1–22:5. These visions of worship guide some of the most frequent songs of the church and help us hear God's call in the midst of many of the scary visions that John sees in Revelation. We'll take some extended time reading Revelation 21, continuing our step-by-step reading of the end of Scripture as God's call to a new beginning for each of us.

SANCTUS ON THE STREETS

In a church basement in South Minneapolis, I took a sip of the best church coffee I've ever had. For some reason churches I've served never make it strong enough. But these two women served the perfect cup—fair trade with plenty of oils floating on the top of the cup. We were gathering at Holy Trinity Lutheran Church in Minneapolis, a congregation that serves the Longfellow neighborhood in robust ways. Two blocks from the Third Precinct of the Minneapolis Police Department, Holy Trinity opened its doors to protestors, bloodied and weeping from tear gas canisters, elbows, shields, and clubs. Following the murder of George Floyd at 38th and Chicago, protestors encircled the police station, which was eventually burned to the ground.

We gathered two years after the Minneapolis uprising at Holy Trinity, an assembly of clergy from different parts of the world, to learn from one another and share our witness together. Pastors from Minneapolis and Leipzig, some of us building on relationships formed years previously, gathered to share stories and listen for calls that emerged in the conversation. Even then, verses from Revelation danced through my brain as we discussed the stories of Christians in Minneapolis and Christians in Leipzig.

It was not a given that Holy Trinity would open its doors to the immediate needs of the neighborhood. But Pastor Ingrid Rasmussen conveyed the story with grace and grit. We had traveled together to Leipzig in 2017 while she was eight months pregnant, delightful friends covering her with umbrellas in the heat of the mid-field festival called a Kirchentag. Three years later, eight months pregnant once again, Ingrid communicated with leaders of Holy Trinity the need to open their doors as a make-shift medic station, offering water and respite to protestors in May of 2020.

"After this I looked, and there in heaven a door stood open!"[1]

Each of the leaders from Holy Trinity shared pieces of the story, but I was captivated by Pastor David Larson-Martinez, who shared memories of keeping fire watch on the church roof, looking at the assembly of protestors and singing of new creation. As bad actors and outside agitators descended on the city, television helicopters circled, and military equipment plowed through the streets, David recalled singing through the liturgy, working his way through every tune of our cranberry-colored hymnal. I was brought to tears as David shared how the liturgy bore witness to the cries from the street below, the shouts of exasperation, chants for a better way, choruses of voices and fists raised—overlooking a neighborhood that would soon be

---

1 Revelation 4:1

overrun by military tanks, fires blazing and cries uplifted, angelic voices rising to heaven.

> Day and night without ceasing they sing,
> "Holy, holy, holy,
> the Lord God the Almighty,
> who was and is and is to come."[2]

David and other leaders from Holy Trinity held an all-night vigil, ensuring that no embers would catch fire on the church, but also bearing witness to the voice of creation itself groaning in this moment for our city and the world. In the cranberry hymnal that Pastor David sang through, the first hundred hymns are variations of this chorus: the *Sanctus* or "holy, holy, holy" appears at the central point of the mass of Western worship practice. Pastor David sang to the heavens, alongside the cries on the streets below, echoing the solidarity of a God who makes a dwelling place among mortals.

Christians sing this chorus the world over, from different traditions, religious expressions, and in countless songs. I grew up singing it as an a cappella hymn tune around the giant oak tree in the yard of our church. I've sung these words with tens of thousands of people filling a stadium with ecstatic prayers. I've sung *atah kadosh* (You Are Holy) alongside Jewish siblings celebrating the High Holy Days of Rosh Hashanah and Yom Kippur. I've lost myself in rich harmonies, crying in Russian "*Svyat, svyat, svyat esi Gospodi*" while performing Rachmaninoff's Orthodox masterpiece before Chicago concert-goers at the Ravinia festival. I've sung these words with fellow Christians on dirt floors in Haiti, in storied German cathedrals, in the Cascade mountains, and in steepled prairie churches.

Known sometimes as the *Sanctus*, its translation in Latin, this threefold proclamation is the constant playlist in the heavenly throne room of Revelation. The word *holy* is so frequently used in Christian circles that it may have lost much of its luster for some of us. But

---

2 Revelation 4:8

here's a reminder: Holy literally means separate. God is holy, set apart, or as some theologians envision, wholly other. God doesn't share characteristics with human beings. As the angels' perpetual chorus sings of God's otherness and God's separation from humanity and creation, the arc of Revelation leans to God making a home among mortals with doors wide open. There is a tension in Revelation between the otherworldly worship services and the chaos that unfolds on earth below. As John is drawn up to the heavenly vantage point, he sees battles and plagues, monsters and murders take place on earth below. But day and night the angels are singing praise to God's sustaining love that lit the heavens, eventually drawing all of creation into an intimate relationship with God, where worship rises from the streets.

Among the three final visions in Revelation is the vision of a new Jerusalem, a city where God resides among mortals:

See, the home of God is among mortals.
He will dwell with them;
they will be his peoples,
and God himself will be with them and be their God.[3]

In Greek, the word *tabernacle* is used twice, to name God's home and the verb of God *dwelling* with the people. In the story of the Exodus, God literally camped (*tabernacled*) with the Hebrew people, traveling with them from the clutches of enslavement into the wilderness and a land of promise beyond. God formed the people of Israel in the wilderness and helped them see the gift of their humanity that had been robbed by the unending demands of Pharaoh's forced labor economy. An entire generation of wandering, and the tabernacle was their place of refuge, of worship, and of belonging. It was where they could trust that God would always be waiting for them, on the mercy seat in the Holy of Holies.

---

3 Revelation 21:3–4

If you need some delightful (or delightfully troubling) bedtime reading, Leviticus has deep concern for maintaining God's holiness through ritual purity of the people and excruciating detail on the construction of the tabernacle. In a complete oversimplification of Leviticus and centuries of rabbinical interpretation, God's holiness is so holy, so separate, so other, that it cannot be met by the typical uncleanliness and ordinariness of human beings. Purification rituals in Leviticus were intended to prevent unintended consequences (like the death of humans or perhaps the end of creation) from coming into contact with God's holiness while remaining unclean. When Isaiah cries that he has unclean lips, the seraphim descend and purify his lips with hot coals so that he can literally eat the divine message. Moses takes his shoes off in God's presence at the burning bush because of the same concern of being too close to God's holiness.

For the people of Jesus's time, the temple of Jerusalem was the representation of the tabernacle, following the directions and specifications given to the people on Mount Sinai. Practices developed that ensured God's holiness would be respected and that provided ways for the Jewish community to purify themselves in the temple system. Jesus's life and ministry testify to the muddying of the waters of clean and unclean, consistently pointing to God's work beyond the neat structures of in and out. Jesus ate with sinners, tax collectors, and prostitutes, agitating legalism in favor of justice for the poor, the widow, and the orphan.

This new tabernacle, however, is not a tent to move about from place to place. It is a holy city, where the streets rejoice from the presence of the living God. Psalm 46 proclaims, "God is in the midst of the city," but the finale of Revelation goes one step further. God's city descends from heaven, not as a comet breathing destruction but as a long-awaited promise, "as a bride adorned for her husband,"[4] opening the gates of the city for a grand celebration. John hears a loud voice from the throne of God that sings of the intimacy that God desires for all of creation. God's home (tabernacle) is among mortals. God

---

4 Revelation 21:2

will dwell (tabernacle) with humans, and we will be God's people. Revelation does not keep the holiness of God locked away, somehow protecting or safeguarding creation. God is on the loose, continuing to preserve everything that is, and in intimate connection with humans with the same love that lit the stars.

Whenever I preside at a funeral I end up quoting this affectionate and loving next verse: "And God shall wipe away all their tears. Death will be no more; mourning and crying and pain will be no more, for the first things have passed away."[5] God doesn't vanish the holy in some rapture but leans in and wipes the tears from all who are looking heavenward for a promise and a blessing. God is not wholly other, alienated from human pain, but weeps alongside us, rages against injustice, wipes our tears, and brings forth a city whose gates are flung wide open. This is not an image of God with aloof power, simply ordaining a clock set in motion, planning and scheming and ordering. It rather shows the love of God who feels the pain of human beings, is deeply moved and grieved by it, sustains the world, and persists in a promise of making all things new.

Again, this city has no temple. When my daughter was three, she needed to visit an ENT because her tonsils needed to be removed. We drove to St. Paul, where a beautiful cathedral stands overlooking the state capitol, its dome stretching higher to heaven than the house of politics. She pointed at it and said, "Daddy! I want to go to that castle!" So, church nerd that I am, and church rat that she is, we finished our appointment with the ENT and took a detour together into the cathedral. I can still hear the intake of her little lungs as she looked skyward, filtered light streaming through the windows, the massive space reminding her of God's grandness. A tiny child, she could sense the awe in the place, could feel the hush of it, and sense the holiness that it reached for. Her wide eyes, her curiosity at the small chapels and lit candles, her questions, and her persistence revealed the holy longing in all of us.

---

5 Revelation 21:4

The new city that descends from heaven has no temple. It has no cathedral. It has no prairie church or mega building. It has no tabernacle. It has no rock band and no stadium seats.

I saw no temple in the city, for its temple is the Lord God the Almighty and the Lamb. And the city has no need of sun or moon to shine on it, for the glory of God is its light, and its lamp is the Lamb. The nations will walk by its light, and the kings of the earth will bring their glory into it. Its gates will never be shut by day—and there will be no night there.[6]

There is no need to mediate God—no priest to receive confession or dispense forgiveness, no prescription of prayer, no penance or repentance, no code or creed or entrance exam. God is in the midst of the city, pulsing a heartbeat of love and sustaining all that was and is and will forever be.

A DIVERSION INTO THE STICKY BITS

If your bones, like mine, are dappled yellow and purple with bruises left by traditions whose marks remain, you may read the penultimate chapter of Revelation and see the lists of folks who are left out of this jubilant city. Your heart may start beating a little bit faster, your skin might prickle, and your memory may conjure certain lists of humans whose sins were too much for an assembly of people.

To be specific, Revelation 21 has two sticky bits. The first was actually a source of hilarity in my youth group growing up. Anytime someone would say something outlandish or stretch the truth about events at school, the group would erupt in a verse to the tune of "Frère Jacques":

Revelation, Revelation.
Twenty-one: eight, twenty-one: eight.

---

6 Revelation 21:22–25

Liars go to hell. Liars go to hell.
Burn, burn, burn. Burn, burn, burn.

Cheery, right? I don't know who brought it to our little church or where the tradition emerged, but I remember singing it again and again. We were right about the citation but missed the point entirely about this section of the Bible. Revelation 21:8 reads: "But as for the cowardly, the faithless, the polluted, the murderers, the sexually immoral, the sorcerers, the idolaters, and all liars, their place will be in the lake that burns with fire and sulfur, which is the second death."

Vice lists are a common occurrence in New Testament literature. In many ways they are a literary device, listing things that people may have nodded along with, perhaps agreeing that there is no place for this kind of mistreatment of God's love and the common bonds of humanity. But many contemporary Christians have turned these lists into ways to highlight the sins of people in our midst. These passages are among the so-called "clobber verses," often used to *clobber* LGBTQIA+ folks in churches and communities. They appear in 1 Corinthians, 1 Timothy, and Jude, where specific Greek words have been translated by committee to wage an intentional cultural war against the achingly slow progress of welcome and affirmation of queer people.[7] While this passage is not included among the most well-trod "clobber" verses, many of us hear in the phrase "sexually immoral" or the word "polluted" entire lists of prohibited behaviors that Evangelical purity culture has insisted upon, including, of course, same-sex relationships.

This passage has been used to provide theological grounding for atrocities throughout Christian history. During the inquisition, heretics were tried by extensive ecclesial courts, tortured, and sentenced to death, fitting clearly in the "faithless" and "idolators" section of Revelation's vice list. Many of these "heretics" were Jews and Muslims who refused the forced conversion that the church required. Witch

---

7 The word *homosexual* is not a word the Bible knows. Rather, interpreters have shaped cultural understanding of these few passages. The documentary film *1946: The Mistranslation that Shifted a Culture* articulates this point. https://www.1946themovie.com.

trials across Europe resulted in tens of thousands of women being sentenced to burning because of the practice of "sorcery" as listed in this section of Revelation. These women were not guilty of practicing any form of witchcraft, but rather many of them were healers, medics, or midwives. Guilty only of some modicum of autonomy, women were tortured, burned, and hung in the United States and across Europe.[8]

Each of these truly demonic movements perverts the overall invitation of this new vision from Revelation. Twelve gates surround the city, representing the twelve tribes of Israel, which "are twelve pearls, each of the gates is a single pearl." St. Peter does not stand in front of the pearly gates of heaven, weeding out the sheep and the goats, allowing entrance to only the most faithful. The final vision of Revelation flings gates wide open: "Its gates shall never be shut by day—and there will be no night there."[9] Even though the chapter concludes with one final, brief vice list ("But nothing unclean will enter it, nor anyone who practices abomination or falsehood, but only those who are written in the Lamb's book of life."[10]), if we follow the key that I introduced at the beginning of the book from Psalm 139, we can trust that God's promise is guiding us through this strange book, beckoning welcome for each and every one of us. If we rise on the wings of the morning, settle at the farthest side of the sea, or make our bed in Sheol, God's hand is guiding each of us, holding us fast, opening the doors of a home for all of creation, where the streets themselves proclaim God's goodness and love.

Each of the words in the vice list have a particular concern with being unclean in the presence of God. As Revelation brings God's presence in immediate connection to human beings, part of this concern may emerge from the ancient fear that God could not be in the presence of uncleanliness. Like the Levitical laws' concern with maintaining

---

8 The BBC produced a remarkable documentary podcast entitled *Witch*. It has helped me relearn the history of witch trials, heresy accusations, and the church's complicity in perpetuating harm against women with significant theological baggage.

9 Revelation 21:25

10 Revelation 21:27

proper distinction, of ordering society and avoiding the destructive nature of chaos, perhaps Revelation is equally concerned with the chaos that emerged from the destruction of the temple, the small but fierce remnant of Jesus followers, and insisting on maintaining their identity in community. A strong sense of communal identity is an essential ingredient to understanding who that early church was, especially in connection to the world around them. They were faced with consistent questions of whether or not to participate in local religious festivals to the emperor. Revelation draws a solid line, insisting that formation in worship is what maintains Christian identity. It criticizes churches who have become lukewarm or who have not resisted fervently enough teachers who might lead them astray. It's possible to read these brief lists as another way to hold this fledgling community together with a strong sense of who they are and who they aren't.

The sticky bits can certainly be stumbling blocks in Revelation, but they are not the entire message. A vice list of the particular concerns of the community in Revelation does not line up perfectly with a list of concerns from today, but they invite us to think about the lines we might draw in the sand. Whose behavior today would preclude participation in the new work that God is doing in our midst? Does the outward vehemence of a congressional leader preclude participation in the communal worship of the Lamb? Does propping up insulin pricing to return investment to shareholders mean that someone is participating in economics that work against the new community God envisions? In our active reading of Revelation, we can poke and prod, wonder and investigate. This list is not our final filter for salvation but an invitation to dance in the streets that shimmer with God's radiance, to see the world through the glittering lights of a city that never sleeps because day and night it is singing praise to the creator.

A WORSHIP REVOLUTION IN LEIPZIG

In 2017, my bishop invited me and a dozen other early-career pastors to visit partners in Leipzig—German pastors and church leaders who wanted to learn alongside Minneapolis counterparts. We participated in much of their commemoration of the 500th anniversary of the Reformation. Living with host families and exploring Leipzig and several other German towns, we attended concerts, exhibits, worship services, and giant festivals. It brought me all the way back to the Christian music festivals I attended as a teenager. Unlike any American revival I experienced, we heard choral music, the best of Bach, and sang the storied hymns of the Reformation. We visited churches that acted like living museums to teach baptism to a largely secular public. We learned about the spirit of reformation that continues around the globe. But the stories of people I met drew me in more than any posterboard exhibit or classical concert.

I stayed with a social worker named Daniel, who lived in a tidy flat in a hip corner of Leipzig. We immediately bonded over music as his son was part of the world-famous Thomanerchor, the boy-choir once conducted by Felix Mendelshon and J. S. Bach before him. We also connected over a glass (or three) of American whiskey, German beer, and a few cigarettes. In some of our conversations late into the hot evenings, Daniel shared stories of time "before the change." Daniel grew up in East Germany, a context I had read about but did not yet understand. Daniel shared that he was a Christian by conviction and by choice. He shared stories of the *Stassi*, the secret police who cultivated sources to report and spy on their neighbors, coworkers, and friends. He wrestled with the decision to look up his secret-police file after the change. Daniel worshipped in the St. Nicolai Church in Leipzig, where peace prayers started among young people, flowing out of a worship gathering and eventually bleeding into the streets in peaceful, candlelit protests.

Daniel was confirmed in the Lutheran Church, the Evangelical church as they call it in Germany. By choosing to be confirmed, Daniel could not attend university because he could not also be a member of the Communist Party. Remembering the curious confirmation students I taught in Minnesota, I wondered how many of them would agree to be confirmed if it meant there was no chance of attending college or advancing a career—certainly a lot fewer. Daniel attended prayer meetings at the St. Nicolai Church in Leipzig, where hundreds, then thousands, then tens of thousands of people gathered in prayer and in song, protesting the occupation, mistreatment, and surveillance of the East German communist government with something they least expected: worship. As Rev. Christian Fuhrer, the preacher who presided over the Monday peace prayers, reflected upon the twentieth anniversary of the fall of the Berlin Wall: "What I saw that evening still gives me the shivers today. And if anything deserves the word 'miracle' at all, then this was a miracle of biblical proportions. We succeeded in bringing about a revolution which achieved Germany's unity, this time without war and military might. It was a peaceful revolution after so much violence and so many wars that we, the Germans, so often started. I will never forget that day."[11]

Seventy thousand people moved toward the center of the city with candles and flowers, prayers and songs. In a triumph of nonviolent resistance, the peaceful protests and prayers in Leipzig led to the fall of the Berlin Wall and the reunification of Germany. These Monday prayer gatherings were a consistent rhythm of the Leipzig Lutheran witness, gathering for months before this momentous occasion, rooting activism and unrest in the lived expression of worship.

Sitting next to Daniel in the same church, singing hymns of the Reformation and stumbling through my poor German, I couldn't help but imagine that his experience of worship was wildly different than my own. Worship was a source of strength in community. Worship was standing in protest. Worship was drawing a line in the sand. Worship was serving a kingdom that stood above the powers and principalities that threatened life in his city. I would imagine that Daniel sees the memories of marching with candles around the walls of Leipzig intermingling with the experience of worship in the vaulted ceiling of that sanctuary.

---

11 Rev. Christian Fuhrer, Interview, National Public Radio, "Voices of a Revolution: Leipzig," November 9, 2009.

CIRCLES OF WORSHIP

Worship is the rhythmic pulse and guiding pattern of Revelation. My Bible teachers in seminary encouraged me to look for the structure of any biblical book. A dense passage from Romans, for example, is constructed to make an argument. It follows a logical progression. If you get lost in the illustration, you might miss the overarching point of the paragraph. As a quite different example, Genesis is stitched together from stories handed down from generation to generation, but it has a clear structure that is laid out in the opening chapter and brought home in the final few verses. In the beginning, God offers a blessing after each day of creation: "It is good." After all of the stories of Abraham, Sarah, and their cantankerous family, at the end of Genesis, Joseph gives a final blessing to his conniving and murderous brothers, returning to the same goodness: "Even though you intended to do harm to me, God intended it for good, in order to preserve a numerous people, as he is doing today."[12] Reading the story of Noah and the ark without this context might lead one to believe that God is a tyrant. (Are pairs of cute animals the reason we share this story with children? The rest of the narrative is decidedly not kid-friendly.) But using the overall structure of the book, we can hear clearly God's intention of goodness, God's grief, and God's promise present in the rainbow to never again flood the earth, but rather work goodness through this strange and often broken family.

Revelation is an entirely different sort of book from Genesis. But it has a clear structure. After the opening sticky notes, worship begins a series of cycles that oscillate between words of judgment—horsemen and wrath, beasts and plagues—and ecstatic visions of worship. Worship is a constant interruption into the drama of the visions that John witnesses, drawing the readers back into the presence of God in the throne room of heaven, where angels are perpetually singing, "Holy, holy, holy," where we hear the promises of God who was and is and will forever be. My seminary teacher, Craig Koester, sketches

---

12 Genesis 50:20

the structure of Revelation in a tradition of interpretation that traces back to the third century, seeing Revelation not as a linear narrative but as a series of overlapping spirals:

> An outline of the book looks like a spiral, with each loop consisting of a series of visions: seven messages to the churches (Rev. 1–3), seven seals (Rev. 4–7), seven trumpets (Rev. 8–11), unnumbered visions (Rev. 12–15), seven plagues (Rev. 15–19), and more unnumbered visions (Rev. 19–22).[13]

A vision of worship occurs at the end of every one of these sections, like the connective tissue of the entire narrative, the driving beat of the song, and the response of the ongoing liturgy.

I didn't grow up in a so-called "liturgical" tradition. When I first stumbled into high church worship, I was completely taken aback. Nadia Bolz-Weber has often joked of the Lutheran calisthenics of standing up and sitting down, crossing, singing, kneeling, responding with short phrases like "hear our prayer," confessing entire paragraphs of the Christian story called creeds, and praying the same prayer that Jesus taught us. As I sat in church as a young child, we sang a few songs, heard a long sermon, and prayed together. While I now see that this tradition has patterns of its own, I've come to appreciate the drama in the liturgical outline of traditional worship services.

In seminary I moonlighted as a choral singer for a variety of choral groups. In the same room that took my daughter's breath away, St. Paul Cathedral, we dressed in black cassocks and processed around the room to an audience of only a few, singing Gregorian chant and renaissance polyphony, and basking in the warm glow of a space that vaulted to the heavens. I grew up highly suspicious of Roman Catholicism with its drama and dance, its flair and flamboyance. But as a budding seminary student I recall being drawn into the drama, the embodied posture of prayer, the perfumed incense

---

13 Craig R. Koester, *Revelation and the End of All Things* (Grand Rapids: Eerdmans, 2001), 39.

and haunting harmony, the costuming of the priests and the depth of tradition that had been practiced for centuries. I remain curious, open, receptive to experiences of worship that involve our whole being—body, mind, and spirit. But worship for the sake of the show can simply be that, a beautiful performance. I long for an experience of worship that does something more.

Worship is a practice that reshapes a community toward God's vision that arrives out of heaven in the final chapter of Revelation. By centering the message of Revelation on seven real churches, and by extension the churches in our lived communities, each heavenly worship service draws us into participation in a worship service for the sake of sustaining the entire planet. We retain hints toward this vision in many of our worship services. In addition to the building blocks of the *Sanctus* and *Agnus Dei* (Lamb of God, who takes away the sin of the world), hymns of the church frequently draw from the poetry of Revelation. In the final verses of Revelation, the temple is God's very presence in the midst of the city, where all the gates are flung wide open, God wipes every tear, and the streets themselves sing the praises of God's love. Worship is the pulse and heartbeat of God's new creation.

FLOSSING IN THE PEWS

It's a favorite joke at gatherings of preachers—no, it doesn't start with a Presbyterian, Methodist, and Lutheran walking into a bar—to cite information about self-reporting attendance at religious services. Many of us are aware of the studies of declining markers of religiousness in the United States. The rise of the "nones" (those marking "none" on a survey about their religious identity) and the decline of organized religion have been the water we're swimming in for decades. And something else fishy happens when Americans report their religious attendance. Americans over-report attendance in church. In 2012, 45 percent of Americans self-reported that they attend church every week.[14] But, when examining

---

14 Shankar Vidantham and Steve Inskeep, "What We Say about Our Religion, and What We Do," *National Public Radio*, October 24, 2012.

their time throughout the week via survey, only half that number show church on their calendar every week. It's like the fateful question in the dentist's office at the six-month check-up, "How often do you brush your teeth? How often do you floss?" Americans over-report flossing at nearly the same clip that they over-report attending church because we think we are the kind of people who attend church, regardless of wherever our rear ends are parked on any given Sunday morning. There are countless books examining why this is, how to remedy it, and which churches are doing a better job of retaining folks in churches, but this, alas, is neither my concern nor the concern of Revelation.

Rather, Revelation has a concern that worship actually matters, that it imparts some lasting effect on the assembly, that it forms us in some way. Nearly every Friday, my spouse treats herself to her favorite drink at our neighborhood coffee chain. She enacts a simple ritual, ordering her beverage on her phone, pulling up to the coffee shop, and walking back with the same cup filled with coffee and dripping with memory, habit, and even emotion. One week the coffee shop struggled to staff early mornings, delaying their opening until 7:30. While this was too late for our early bird to get to school on time, she commented on the large number of people who were waiting in line for the opening bell. This lapse in her routine threw off her day and her week, while others would not even begin their day without their preferred order. Contemporary society forms us in very specific ways, influencing our values and desires, our longings and our loves.[15] Advertisers shape our feelings and emotions, cultivating a longing for the next iPhone or trending sweater. Influencers on TikTok or Instagram connect with their audiences by showcasing a life that is authentic or enviable or hilarious or honest. Haptics and micro transactions elicit dopamine responses, literally herding us toward an intended aim of more sales and more market share.

---

15 James K. A. Smith describes this phenomenon quite well in *You Are What You Love: The Spiritual Power of Habit.*

For some Christians, worship is something that we do on Sunday morning. For other Christians, worship is a once-a-month or once-a-year engagement. In one hour, we sing songs, recite prayers, light candles, read from Scripture, hear a sermon, and perhaps taste a cracker and sip of juice. But worship is also something that happens all around us in the culture. Simple rituals of our daily existence form liturgies and litanies, scripts that express our lived spirituality more than our attendance card for church. How can the liturgy enacted in one hour on Sunday morning have any impact on these contemporary competing liturgies?

Apocalyptic literature breaks open our imagination and wakes us up to the possibility of God moving in remarkable ways before our very eyes. If we visited church and were whisked away into the clouds to see a glassy sea and the throne-room of God, perhaps we would attend more often. Or perhaps we would run away and tell no one, like the disciples on Easter morning. By cycling again and again around worship, Revelation insists that we are formed by this communal act of alternative imagination.

In what other assembly of people do we sing together, sharing breath and melody and rhythm? What if the next school board meeting began with singing a song that affirmed the belovedness of everyone in the room? Communal worship can shape our imagination just like Pastor David singing through the hymnal from a rooftop above Longfellow or Daniel singing songs and lighting candles around the city walls of Leipzig. If Karl Marx believed religion to be the opiate of the masses, then the religion he critiqued looked nothing like Longfellow or Leipzig or the vision streaming out of Revelation. Yet many of our worship services are uninspired. Many fall flat. Many weary pastors are afraid to voice contemporary concerns in prayers or sermons because of the polarization in their pews.

But liturgy is the work of the people. It isn't performed by a select few standing up on Sunday mornings. Worship is a heartbeat of practice for communities that gather all over the world, trusting that

God is still moving in our midst. Worship can halt empires. Worship uproots systems and structures. Worship grounds us in a tradition that stretches for generations before us and will last for generations into the future. Revelation believes that worship matters to our existence as a community that follows Jesus. It doesn't speculate on what it should look or sound like, but it insists that we make it the regular rhythm of our lives.

5

Heaven on Earth: We Need It Now

In this chapter, we will not be looking specifically at one section of Revelation. Rather, we will confront one of the more pervasive misreadings of Revelation: rapture theology. There isn't a section of Revelation that walks through the rapture, which should be our first hint of the miss in the interpretation. However, we'll find that the promises of God in Revelation 22 echo from the end of Scripture to its very beginning in Genesis 2. I encourage you to read these Bible bookends as we dive into the deep end of end-times misinterpretation together.

Bono gets the credit for the title of this chapter. I've never seen "Peace on Earth" from U2's album *Nothing You Can't Leave Behind* on a Christmas hit list or heard it on the pop-up Christmas radio stations I start listening to in September (for real). But in my not-so-humble opinion the song deserves its place next to Nat King Cole's open fire, Mariah Carey's wish come true, or Bing's sleigh bells in the snow. Written in response to the Omagh bombing in 1998, the opening line sounds more like a prayer in Edge's paired-down recording from 2023. With simple acoustic guitar that recalls the campfires of my youth, it aches for the promises of Scripture to be made real, here and now. Intoning the Christmas blessing of "peace on earth" over the violence of the Troubles in Northern Ireland or the global flashpoint of 9/11, the song has been described as agnostic by critics,[1] but it actually holds the tension of some deeply theological pondering. It points to the core of the question for our text at hand. Does Revelation predict a time in the future or call us to task today? Does it speak of heaven beyond or here on earth? There or here? Now or later?

I can recall this moment in spring 2020 when the post-apocalyptic shows and movies that I had so enjoyed started losing their flavor. *The Handmaid's Tale* felt too close to reality with the policies spinning out of Bible Belt states. Matt Damon wasn't wearing a mask on *Contagion* in suburban Minnesota, but I was. In search of toilet paper, it felt like rationing might have been a good idea. Post-apocalyptic fiction relies on a common assumption that the time that these stories are describing is other than right now. But, the best stories help us see how we might slip into apocalypse in a sneeze of history, a gasp of misfortune, or a guffaw of political rhetoric. My discomfort in watching these newly disquieting tales came from the notion that we were eerily close to those apocalyptic visions.

In theological terms, an alternative time, often in the future, is also the gambit of apocalyptic literature in the Bible, like Revelation. Does Revelation orient us toward the future or toward the present? Yes. Does Revelation orient us toward heaven or toward earth? Yes. Welcome to the possibly maddening doublespeak of theology. There is a term in the Protestant tradition called dialectic theology that relies on the mystery and truth present in these paradoxes. For example, Lutherans (who still tolerate me for some reason!) believe that Christians are *simultaneously* sinners and saints, in the same breath, at the same moment. Another famous dialectic is found in one of Martin Luther's earliest texts: "A Christian is a perfectly free lord of all, subject to none. A Christian is a perfectly dutiful servant

---

1 Niall Stokes, *U2: Into the Heart—The Stories Behind Every Song* (New York: Thunder's Mouth Press, 2005).

of all, subject to all."[2] The dialectic helps us see the honesty of either end of the pole, a great theological judo move for our us-and-them, zero-sum-game, polarized world of politics these days. It helps us see shades of grey and mysteries that can't easily sit on either side of the aisle.

When we're talking about Revelation, we are often drawing on a sub-discipline of theology called eschatology. I know we're diving a bit into the weeds here, but just think of all the trivia answers you'll have next time you join your compatriots at the local theological pub trivia night. (Wait, you won't meet me there?) Eschatology is concerned with the end of all things, the end of the story, the end goal of God's love in the world. It wonders where we're headed. It asks the questions of when and where and how God is moving the world. For the liturgically minded folks, the Apostle's Creed confesses that Jesus "is seated at the right hand of the Father almighty; from thence he will come to judge the living and the dead." Eschatology wonders about that return of Jesus to judge the living and the dead. A central theme of eschatological thinking is the idea of "already and not yet." We live in the tension, on the invisible tightrope between God's reign envisioned at the end of Revelation and the not-yet reality that our world continues to be broken, full of pain, fear, sorrow, war, and devastation. As Christians, we inherit God's compelling vision of tomorrow even though we also know we are not there yet. As Paul writes, we see "through a glass dimly"[3] and cannot understand or comprehend or approximate the vision, but it breaks into our world nonetheless in God's ongoing and persistent promise. The love that lit the stars reaches from the end of all things to surprise us with possibility and hope.

Popular apocalyptic works move us in an "already and not yet" kind of way. By calling out to the future, looking ahead at an often unnumbered year ahead of our own, these stories call back with urgency for our own situation. When we see the zombie apocalypse

---

2 Martin Luther, *On the Freedom of a Christian.*
3 1 Corinthians 13:12

in *The Last of Us*, we clearly understand that our world isn't as bad as the wasteland that Pedro Pascal saunters through, but we can imagine it slipping quickly into something resembling those terrible images. *The Handmaid's Tale* displays a world that looks extremely unlike our own in some ways. But through a couple of political missteps, crises that we don't expect, and heightened divisions already fracturing our communal life together, many could envision our nation slipping quickly toward it. Before we dig into the questions of when and where Revelation is pulling us, we have one more vision to read at the end of the end of the last book of the Bible—a tale of a great garden in the middle of God's city.

GARDEN TO GARDEN (FROM BEGINNING TO END)

As a child of Evangelicalism, Rob Bell built bridges for me from fundamentalism into something else entirely. When my faith was little more than tattered threads spilling out of a cardboard box, his books and videos helped me envision a faith that was more imaginative and real. I remember watching his *Nooma* videos for the first time and encountering a preacher who wasn't afraid of asking the questions that were off the table in youth group. In one of these short films, he slowly planted two trees while talking through the camera into my questions and doubts. Starting with the Garden of Eden and the tree at the center of the garden and reaching all the way to the end of the Bible, perhaps the end of everything, he said that the story of creation was a story of what happened between two trees. Garden to garden. Paradise to paradise.

In a typical telling of this story, the Garden of Eden was perfect, where humanity had everything that they could ever need. Yet the serpent spoiled it all, leading Eve and Adam (with a little raised eyebrow that Eve sinned first) to sin against God and rupture the perfection that God intended for all of creation. The work of God through the people of Israel and the person of Jesus, then, is to bring humanity and creation back from the brokenness of that original sin and the original sin that lives in all of us. A whole lot of hubbub around a piece of fruit, isn't it?

Perhaps you grew up with a theology that draws from this story an understanding of total depravity or original sin, where the cause of the cross and the judgment of the Bible is placed squarely on the mantle of our shoulders as human beings. Perhaps you have sat through Good Friday services where you were asked to bear the weight of the cross as the ones who crucified Jesus. Revelation calls us into a different reading of the arc of God's work in creation and among humanity. The end is the beginning (is the end is the beginning). Revelation sees God's victory revealed in the nonviolent presence of Jesus, the lamb who was slain. But first, I have a few bones (three to be exact) to pick with that classic telling of the garden story.[4]

Bone 1: Ask Multiple Voices the Right Questions

The Garden of Eden is actually the second of two creation stories, revealing multiplicity of voices from the very first pages of Scripture. These stories help us understand our role in creation. They are not science textbooks depicting how the rocks were formed and how creatures lived and died and became extinct. If we go looking at Genesis for those kinds of answers, we'll always find ourselves off course. We've discussed the first creation story, where patterns of seven upon seven upon seven reveal a deep structure and beauty to God's creation. In this first creation account, God sings a blessing over the world, calling every aspect of creation "good" and setting apart the seventh day as a breath of sacred rest. The first story describes humanity as the pinnacle of creation, the only part of creation called "*very* good" and tasked with having "dominion" or *responsibility* for creation.

---

4 If you want far more than three bones, read the amazing book by Rita Nakashima Brock and Rebecca Ann Parker, *Saving Paradise: How Christianity Traded Love of This World for Crucifixion and Empire* (Boston: Beacon Press, 2009).

The second story brings the first human (*ha adam* in Hebrew literally means the earth-creature and is certainly not a proper name, though don't tell Adam Levine so he doesn't quit *The Voice*) alongside God to tend the garden, to till creation, to name the creatures that emerge. In this second, more earthy account, God shapes the first human from the dirt, breathing into them the breath of life. Each of these stories has different answers to our questions of why we are here, to our questions of how to work alongside God in this good creation.

Bone 2: Don't Blame Eve

First of all, God gives the instructions to Adam, "You may freely eat of every tree of the garden, but of the tree of the knowledge of good and evil you shall not eat, for in the day that you eat of it you shall die."[5] Eve isn't even created (or named) yet! The woman (not Eve until the end of the story!) eventually hears God's message, either from Adam or from the Lord God, who walks through the garden for a stroll on occasion. The serpent approaches the woman, and she responds with God's edict to refrain from the fruit in the center of the garden. Because the serpent is "more crafty than any other animal," the creature offers a promise, "you will not die, for God knows that when you eat of it your eyes will be opened, and you will be like God, knowing good and evil."[6] The man and woman both eat, and God responds with clear consequences for the serpent, the woman, and the man. Christian theology and history have repeatedly blamed Eve as the carrier of sin, blaming women for the sin of men. Witch trials, inquisitions, and in more recent times purity culture police women's bodies under an absurd presumption of preventing male temptation while perpetuating cycles of sexualization and abuse.[7] Reacting against gains for women in the public square, the complementarian movement doubles down on the hierarchy of men

---

5 Genesis 2:16–17

6 Genesis 2:4–5

7 Emily Joy Allison, *#ChurchToo: How Purity Culture Upholds Abuse and How to Find Healing* (Minneapolis: Broadleaf Books, 2021).

in the church and the world,[8] insisting that women submit to men in their "complementary" role to the leadership (called headship in their system) of men in the family, church, and world. We should actively resist these narratives because they are harmful to women (and men) and because they are completely unbiblical.

Bone 3: The Serpent Isn't Satan

I was always told that the serpent is the Devil, Satan, the Accuser, the evil one, who caused all of the destruction of Eden, who cursed the first humans with pain in childbirth and toil to till the land. I was told that the Devil caused evil to enter the world, was present when Cain killed Abel, and is always prowling for us, ready to devour us with behavior that will lead to our own destruction. We'll get into Satan in more depth in the next chapter. But, for now, it is important to see that the serpent is a trickster of a creature. The serpent isn't the source of all evil, just a trickster who got the humans to eat fruit that they shouldn't have. Tricksters show up throughout Genesis. Jacob tricks his brother Esau out of his inheritance and is later tricked by his Uncle Laban. This is dysfunctional behavior, but is it the cause of all evil and war and chaos in the world? I'm not so sure. By aligning this singular mistake and the ensuing consequences with the source of all evil, we risk further perpetuating the sin of Eve, aligning women with flesh and sin.

∗∗∗

We don't just pick bones with Scripture because it's fun or an interesting academic exercise. By wrestling with what we have inherited, we can confront misuses of these texts, understand more deeply

---

8 The complementarian movement is very much white Evangelical insider speak. Books and articles and conferences attempt to reclaim the "complementary" role of women and men in society. Under its reactionary and harmful theology, women want a heroic husband who will work to support the family, and men are charged with being the spiritual leaders of the family unit. Rather then being created equal (egalitarian) this theology espouses male authority over all things in the family because they are "created" to be this way.

the original contexts in which they were written, and listen more carefully for the living voice of God whispering in our midst. It's like learning the scales in music and then moving on toward more complex pieces. Revelation (and the rest of Scripture) are constantly calling back to the stories in Genesis and Exodus (and Leviticus, Numbers, and Deuteronomy). If we get the stories wrong to begin with, we might end up playing an entirely different song. Try randomly turning the pegs on a piano and then go and play a piece of Bach—it won't sound very "well-tempered" and certainly won't make any wedding procession playlists.

Revelation returns to Eden as God recreates the gift of that primordial paradise where Eve and Adam lived in a peaceable kingdom. After a new creation is inaugurated, after the new Jerusalem descends, where God dwells in the midst of the city, we are offered one final vision of promise—the river of the water of life. Right through the center of the city, a river flows from the throne of God. The tree of life, if the references to Eden weren't clear enough yet, straddles the river on either side. Echoing the structure of creation with twelves (rather than sevens), it produces twelve kinds of fruit and offers fruit every month (twelve upon twelve). But every piece of this tree is useful and effective as "the leaves of the tree are for the healing of the nations."[9] The number twelve refers to the twelve tribes of Israel, but twelve also expands the circle to include nations beyond those twelve tribes. Earlier in Revelation, the followers of Jesus are counted as both 144 thousand and a great multitude: "I heard the number of those who were sealed, one hundred forty-four thousand, sealed out of every tribe of the people of Israel . . . After this I looked, and there was a great multitude that no one could count, from every nation, from all tribes and peoples and languages, standing before the throne and before the Lamb, robed in white, with palm branches in their hands."[10] All nations are healed in this paradise from the oppressive regime of the Roman Empire but also from the forces of

---

9 Revelation 22:2
10 Revelation 7:4, 9

empire that continue in our present moment. Multiples of twelve remember the original covenant with Abraham: "I will make of you a great nation, and I will bless you and make your name great, so that you will be a blessing." The multiples of twelve, both 144 (which my daughter will confirm is twelve squared) and 144 thousand, envision the ever-expanding unfolding of God's love for *all* the nations.

It is important to pause here and speak to an incredibly harmful interpretation of the 144 thousand who come from the twelve tribes of Israel. Evangelical Christianity has had a long history of supporting the state of Israel for incredibly hurtful and antisemitic reasons. I am completing this manuscript during a horrendous loss of life in Israel and Gaza. After celebrating High Holy Days, as I do every year with a local synagogue in Minneapolis, and commemorating those who died in the Yom Kippur War of 1973, the very next week brought radio stories of entire families being murdered and children kidnapped by Hamas, then seeing a city of two million people bombed into rubble with a nearly uncountable loss of life. I will not be speaking into this conflict here, but I want to highlight that Christian Zionism is not a way to support our Jewish neighbors or even the state of Israel. It articulates a vision of end-times that stitches Daniel and Revelation together into an entirely fictional account of the end of the world where Jews are converted and then disappear before the end of the play, leaving none to inherit the beautiful vision that God has for all nations of the earth. Christian Zionism twists both the message of Revelation and the Hebrew prophetic tradition. It purports to be supportive of Israel while actively praying for and anticipating an endgame where Jewish people do not inherit the glorious vision at the end of Revelation. In its overtures for supporting policies across the globe, it is actually deeply antisemitic and dangerous.[11] 144 thousand from every tribe in Israel is not limited to only Jewish

---

11 Barbara Rossing dedicates a chapter to challenging the end-times obsession of Christian Zionism in her book, *The Rapture Exposed: The Message of Hope in the Book of Revelation* (New York: Basic Books, 2004). Steven Sizer also has written a history of the movement in *Christian Zionism: Road-map to Armageddon?* (New York: Wipf & Stock, 2021).

people or a select few faithful Christians. It is an expansive vision of blessing for the entire world, of welcome into the new Eden, where all nations are healed by the sustainer of the cosmos.

When the ancients heard this description of a new Eden, the final vision of promise at the end of Revelation, they would have heard the model coming right from Ezekiel 47, where a garden grows from a great river flowing from the temple. Living water flowing from the presence of God at the center of the city, the river in Ezekiel's vision is too large to cross and teaming with life: "Wherever the river goes, every living creature that swarms will live, and there will be very many fish once these waters reach there. It will become fresh, and everything will live where the river goes."[12] The river is the source of all life, all creation, all possibility and promise. John nearly quotes directly from this passage in his description of the tree: "On the banks, on both sides of the river, there will grow all kinds of trees for food. Their leaves will not wither nor their fruit fail, but they will bear fresh fruit every month, because the water for them flows from the sanctuary. Their fruit will be for food and their leaves for healing."[13]

But there is a stark contrast between the source of the river and the life that flows out of it. In Ezekiel, the source is the temple, the place where worship and God's presence are aligned in a powerful way for the people of Israel. But the role of the temple is redefined in Revelation "for its temple is the Lord God the Almighty and the Lamb."[14] God is sustaining all of creation with life through the Lamb, Jesus Christ. God is healing the nations through the life that springs forth from the river and the garden around it. God is in the midst of the city, flinging wide the gates and welcoming all into the presence of God's goodness. Each of these unfolding visions at the end of Revelation helps Christians orient ourselves to the world around us, much like the original creation stories. They help us understand the

---

12 Ezekiel 47:9
13 Ezekiel 47:12
14 Revelation 21:22

role of Christians and the church, our corporate worship, and finally answer our questions for this chapter: There or here? Now or later?

THERE OR HERE?

Along I-94 in beautiful central Minnesota, past countless regal red Dairy Queens, there is a billboard that reads, "Where are you going?" On the left are fluffy cumulus clouds with blue block letters, "Heaven." On the right, you guessed it, are flames and yellow letters, "Hell." A junction betwixt these words is a single conjunction, whose function couldn't be clearer: we are either going to a happy home in the heavens *or* a fiery torment in hell below. With a simple, toll-free call to the number on the bottom of the billboard, I'm sure I could determine my final destination.

I didn't grow up handing out tracts, but I bumped into them in all the usual spots—stadium revivals, Bible camps, and Christian music festivals. These small pamphlets, like the billboard I see regularly, try to force the hard questions on passersby. I don't know if they are the most effective form of evangelism, and likely Evangelicals would agree with me here, but they were everywhere growing up. They orient us to the life beyond, in the by-and-by, and the pressing ongoing question of what happens when we die. This is a compelling question for Americans, 73 percent of whom articulate some form of belief in heaven as the afterlife.[15]

Christian traditions and people of faith tend to be either heaven-bent or earthbound. Heaven-bent traditions might emphasize personal piety, morality, prayer, and study of Scripture. On the other end of a religious spectrum, earthbound traditions emphasize the power of God's action in the world—mission organizations who either share the gospel or share essential needs or some combination

---

15 Pew Research, "Views on the afterlife: Majorities of U.S. adults say they believe in heaven, hell," November 23, 2021, https://www.pewresearch.org /religion/2021/11/23/views-on-the-afterlife/

of the two, and political organizations that work to see their values in elected officials and in the laws of the land. Of course, most of us are a mixture of the two, but it is helpful to tease out this tension in our work of faith because how we read Revelation is often influenced by where we sit on this spectrum.

One more historical example is the difference between mendicant and monastic traditions. For the Lutherans who have come to tolerate my unorthodox faith (and lengthy preaching), I have two party tricks. The first is that they are surprised to hear that I've never been confirmed (even though I've confirmed hundreds of young people). The second is when I tell them that their beloved Martin Luther was not a monk. The strange haircut and the brown robes solidify in contemporary imagination this German monk who spent his life translating the Bible and working for reform of the church. But Martin Luther was a Franciscan friar, a mendicant rather than a monastic tradition. Mendicants tend toward the earthbound side of the holy orders, and Luther was deeply spiritually informed by the practice of begging in city streets in order to feed the poor in the community. While mendicants are more earthbound, monastic traditions could be considered more heaven-bent. Thomas Merton was a Trappist monk who taught early traditions of what we might now call mindfulness. Merton practiced regular silence, stillness, and solitude, cultivating spirituality that was spacious enough to engage in the world meaningfully. You'll of course notice that both of these teachers of the faith incorporated both sides of the spectrum. Luther studied and prayed long hours, even though he knew that his salvation was not determined by these spiritual expressions. Merton on the other hand was an activist for peace in a time of great conflict, cultivating relationship with Thich Nhat Hanh, a Vietnamese Zen Buddhist monk, as part of his ongoing activism against the war in Vietnam.

In the tradition I was raised in, faith was largely heaven-bent. At the risk of oversimplification, much of our religious practice was aimed at certainty of heaven. The Lutherans around me are also often scandalized by the notion that I was baptized as an adolescent. I have the clearest memory of the conversation when our motorcycle-riding, fiery preacher softened to speak with me quietly about why I wanted to be baptized. Baptism was an outpouring of my individual faith, the believer's prayer I prayed when I was young, the personal relationship with Jesus that I tended in prayer and study of Scripture, and the confession of faith that I gave to the pastor and the church before I was baptized. Baptism wasn't a ticket into heaven. It was a sign of the faith that I was tending in my constant practice of Christian expression, working out my faith in fear and trembling.

The Evangelical landscape also has plenty of earthbound expressions. As we've already discussed, the *Left Behind* series brought the concept of the rapture into mainstream Christian discourse. It was part of a Christian media mechanism that used all the tools at its disposal to market Christian identity and belonging. Most Christians in the 1980s, 1990s, and 2000s in the United States have consumed, bumped into, or participated in this movement at some point: the growth of the Christian contemporary music industry, the revivals of Billy Graham, the Promise Keepers, Focus on the Family, the Moral Majority, and other politically aligned movements. Even the Motion Picture Association of America (MPAA), who rates films, television, and streaming offerings to this day began as an extension of this movement in contemporary American society.[16]

But Evangelicalism isn't the only heaven-bent faith tradition. Like the churches in the beginning of Revelation, this vision cuts both ways. Liberal or mainline traditions have similar approaches with different goals. On the earthbound side, progressives favor Jesus's call in Matthew 25 that those nearest the kingdom of heaven are those

---

16 While this book isn't ultimately focused on defining or tracing the contours of the Evangelical movement, it is important for folks to understand just how pervasive it is. Because most Christians don't know enough about the various interpretations of these corners of Scripture, it is relatively easy for rapture theology and other harmful interpretations to creep into media that they consume.

who are clothing the naked, feeding the hungry, and visiting the sick and imprisoned. Political activism is for the sake of "the least of these" in order to follow Jesus's teachings clearly. On the heaven-bent side of the liberal Protestant poll is a teddy-bear Jesus, psychobabble, and *Chicken Soup for the Soul.*

Perhaps I'm touching a nerve for some who love the neat and tidy faith represented in these short stories gathered near the turn of the century. In one of my first offices as a professional Christian leader, I needed to make room for my book collection. Like any good English major turned seminary nerd, I love my books. Sometimes I stand up when I'm thinking and imagine a conversation with various volumes, thinking through what they would have to say about the lesson I'm preaching or the question asked in the Bible study or the internal conflict at hand. But when I entered my office for the very first time I found every volume of *Chicken Soup for the Soul* in existence: three volumes for teenagers, several marked specifically for Christians, a few of the original published in 1993, and several more marketed for dog and cat lovers respectively. What would someone do with so many volumes of *Chicken Soup for the Soul*? I mean, doesn't the soul need a well-rounded diet? Some grains, a bit of protein, perhaps something a bit spicy every now and again like a Thai curry or a steaming bowl of pho. If you don't know the series, each volume contains short entries that are syrupy-sweet, always spinning a tale to make you feel warm and good inside, like a hot bowl of chicken soup. But they fall flat without dimensions of complexity, real-world concerns, or ordinary crises. The fluffier versions of heaven-bent mainline traditions emphasize feel-good stories of Jesus who is always loving us and never has anything hard to say. They encourage without conviction. A chicken-soup Jesus is drawn from various corners of Scripture that highlight the love of Christ without the indictment or challenge. Dietrich Bohnhoeffer, a theologian and pastor who was executed by the Third Reich for his participation in a plot to assassinate Hitler, would call this *cheap* grace. Revelation actively resists this fluffy, teddy-bear Jesus, calling such churches tepid communities that lack the fire of the Spirit.

Revelation resists the temptation toward either a heaven-bent or earthbound faith expression. It insists on a change of perspective when it comes to our imaginations of heaven and hell. As we've already discussed, God's home is among mortals in the conclusion of Revelation. Heaven on earth is the end vision of God's love in the world. As Bono's lyrics lament the yawning gap between God's promise and our reality, Revelation forces us to wrestle with our apathy at empire or complicity in harming creation. We are formed in ongoing worship of Jesus, the lamb who redefines victory, belonging, and peace. The billboard might be an effective device for those of us speeding down the interstate, but it completely misses the message that Revelation is preaching. God is sustaining all that was, is, and will forever be. Rapture enthusiasts or mainline teddy-bear Jesus types may try to pull Revelation toward a heaven-bent interpretation, but the text doesn't allow it. We've been reading, step by step, the end of this book, where God's commitment is made abundantly clear. God continues to sustain creation, you and me, healing the nations, and loving the world with abandon.

Whether we grew up in mainline Protestant or Evangelical circles, our imaginations of heaven are formed in a variety of places. Hymns sing, "Some glad morning, when my life is o'er, I'll fly away. To a home on God's celestial shore, I'll fly away." One of my late grandmother's favorites, "Blessed Assurance," draws inspiration from the ongoing worship in Revelation, "This is my story, this is my song, praising my savior all the day long." But the second verse betrays a theology that echoes in countless (mis)interpretations of Revelation, "Perfect communion, perfect delight, visions of rapture now burst on my sight." Rapture is a response to both questions: "here or there?" and "now or later?" But, alas, rapture appears nowhere in the book of Revelation. Wait. Did you just read that? Indeed, rapture appears nowhere in the book of Revelation. And it is only referred to once in all of Scripture (outside of a few people who ascend heavenward, like Jesus and Elijah). If you are unfamiliar with the idea of a rapture, it is the belief that God will whisk away all the believers in Christ before a time of tribulation and the end of the world. The idea of a rapture is a relatively recent innovation in Christian theology and is a direct answer to the eagerness of some to find their way to heaven.

VISIONS OF RAPTURE NOW BURST ON MY SIGHT

My friend Tim is one of the most gifted musicians I know. Melodies dance off his fingers as if they're conjured from thin air. If we aren't swapping recommendations of graphic novels or sci-fi streaming, we share stories of emerging from fundamentalism in adulthood. Tim's uncle was a fairly famous filmmaker in the Evangelical world. When I shared with him that I was writing on Revelation, the whole story came out.

His uncle made a low-budget movie that turned into a Christian cultural phenomenon in 1972. Before the *Left Behind* series formed Evangelicals in my generation, *A Thief in the Night* was produced for only $68,000 and brought in a whopping $4.2 million within the first decade of its release. Viewable in its entirety on YouTube, the opening scene uses Hitchcock's tools of horror to get under the viewers' skin immediately. A ticking alarm clock beats persistently while a radio wakes a young woman to reports of millions of people disappearing twenty-five minutes earlier. Close-quarter shots leave us nowhere to avert our gaze in an incredibly unsettling opening scene. The young woman finds her husband vanished with his shaver still buzzing in the sink. We hear only her scream as the reporter concludes the radio story with a haunting quotation from Jesus: "But of that day and hour knoweth no man, no, not the angels of heaven, but my Father only."[17]

I love movies. And I love movies that mean something, that invite reflection and conversation. But Christian films regularly fall flat for me. This isn't a criticism if you absolutely love the latest season of *The Chosen*. I often feel, however, that many of these films are trying to lead the audience in one direction, rather than allowing for multiple

---

17 Matthew 24:36, KJV

perspectives. *The Thief in the Night* is a classic example. Its goal is quite clear—to scare a generation into clarity of their faith, values, and morals.[18] The *Left Behind* series uses the tools of the action and disaster films of the turn of the century, whereas *A Thief in the Night* uses all of the tools in the classic horror toolbox to frighten viewers. The doomsday clock at the beginning, the tight cinematography that creeps under your skin, campy special effects, and conspiracy theories about the United Nations all contribute to the horror of the film, instilling a sense of fear that doesn't end when the credits roll.

I recall distinctly the feeling in the pit of my stomach when people wandered into the local Cold Stone Creamery where I worked in one of my first jobs. Serving sweets mixed on a frozen slab of granite, a few of them had dark smudges on their forehead. I couldn't figure out what these smudges were. Some people wore the smudges, and others didn't. My anxiety sank deep as I remembered the mark of the beast and pondered when I would be asked to wear such a mark. Turns out that it was Ash Wednesday, a day where liturgical Christians mark their foreheads with ashes in the sign of the cross to remind them of their mortality. This couldn't be further from the mark of the beast. Whenever I couldn't find my family as a child in the grocery store or from the laundry room, I would wonder if they had been raptured and I'd been left behind. I kid about it today (sick sense of humor, I know) only because the feeling still lingers. Rapture anxiety is what many post-Evangelical folks call it as corners of Christianity continue to have public conversations on podcasts and TikTok videos about religious trauma.

Rapture theology induces fear. The theology itself is a horror film. Confess your sins, repent of your misdeeds, and turn to God because Jesus could return at any moment, like a thief in the night. Do you want to be raptured with the people you love? Or do you want to be left behind? Like the DARE program tried to scare a generation away

---

18 Pierce Baugh, "This Horrifying Rapture Movie Changed Christian Cinema Forever," *Collider*, https://collider.com/a-thief-in-the-night-christian-movie/

from using drugs, emboldened by the multimedia empire of Evangelicalism, rapture theology influences "a whole range of conservative political issues including anti-abortion, anti-homosexuality, anti-environmentalism, militarism, and Middle East policy, was well as opposition to the United Nations."[19] The message is quite clear: fall in line with the policies, moralities, and principles of faith or risk being left behind and facing the terror that will follow. The honest truth, however?[20] The rapture was invented just shy of 1900 in England, shipped to the United States, grew like wildfire through the growth of fundamentalism, was amplified by popular media from the 1970s through the 2000s, and continues as a guiding post in Evangelical communities who are already prone to conspiracy theories like the Q-Anon phenomenon. The word "rapture" appears nowhere in the Bible, and the concept is nowhere in Revelation.

Its basis is found in one passage in Paul's first letter to the Thessalonians (also where the idea of an anti-Christ appears): "Then we who are alive, who are left, will be *caught up* in the clouds together with them to meet the Lord in the air, and so we will be with the Lord forever."[21] This is the only verse that explicitly envisions followers of Jesus in "visions of rapture." The Latin translation of the word *caught up* is *raptio*, and this is the only place in Scripture that the original Greek word appears. John Nelson Darby formalized this new innovation in theology between the 1850s and 1870s and drew from one other apocalyptic text to answer the question of when Jesus will return. Based on three verses in Daniel, Darby invents an idea of epochs in history called *dispensations*. With some creative

---

19 Barbara Rossing, *The Rapture Exposed: The Message of Hope in the Book of Revelation,* (New York, Basic Books, 2005), 43.

20 I am speeding through this. It may induce a bit of whiplash if you haven't interrogated your understanding of the rapture. If that is the case, I strongly encourage you to read Barbara Rossing's book in full. *The Rapture Exposed* traces the entire history of this movement, its impact in contemporary society, and calls us to find a more fulfilling view of Revelation. I am indebted to Dr. Rossing's work.

21 1 Thessalonians 4:17

mathematics and various multiples of seven, the church conveniently lives before the final epoch, when Jesus will return first to whisk the faithful away and a second time to judge the living and the dead. Dispensationalists, as these folks are hence called, rely on a strict definition of biblical prophecy as predicting something that will happen in the future. Some of these prophecies are fulfilled in Jesus and others are awaiting fulfilment to this day. When Jesus gets a little apocalyptic in the Bible, it isn't to make a point about the world in front of him and invite us to do the same. It is an unfulfilled prophecy that we are awaiting in our penultimate epoch of history.

If your eyes are glazing over, I completely get it. I share only the tip of the proverbial iceberg because the calculations of those who follow this stuff are far more complicated than what I've outlined here. For our book, Revelation, we see a few very strange numbers, including a couple that matter quite a bit to the rapture-furious. We've discussed already the number seven, which appears all over Revelation. It is the number of wholeness, of the sabbath, of God's ongoing commitment and love for creation. But the rapture inaugurates, you guessed it, seven years of complete devastation called the tribulation. After the church is whisked away, the battles, plagues, and beasts of Revelation will unfold on earth over seven years. Using math that would not earn a passing grade in my daughter's fourth grade class, they combine two numbers in Revelation 11:2–3: "they will trample over the holy city for forty-two months. And I will grant my two witnesses authority to prophesy for one thousand two hundred sixty days, wearing sackcloth." Of course these numbers are snatched, perhaps *raptured* directly out of context, where Revelation has no discussion of tribulation in this section of the book that alternates, as we've discussed, between visions of challenge and beautiful never-ending worship services.

But, as I have been sharing bits of the end of Revelation first, we can begin to see that the end is the beginning. God is not abandoning creation. God is not allowing creation to destroy itself. God is not turning creation over to destructive forces at all. God's persistent promise is to sustain creation through all that was, and is, and is to come. All of God's power and victory is lodged in the awareness that the creator of the universe is not done with us yet. In the strange up-side-down power of Jesus, the lamb who was slain, we catch a glimpse of a power that upends all of our understanding of the world. It's a promise of God's goodness in, with, and under everything that was, is, and is to come. In a word: always.

SUSTAINER OF THE WORLD

Anytime I list the things I want to do before I die, the top ten are all locations, places to visit and experience. I had ample opportunity to travel as I grew up, but I am hankering for more, always living vicariously through friends who return from an adventure. My friend Peter recently returned from another trip to Egypt, where he spent time at St. Catherine's monastery in the Sinai desert. Peter took members of our congregation to experience this holy site, to take time away standing near the mountain that Moses climbed to receive the Ten Commandments. One of the most famous images of Jesus from all of history is found in this monastery, nestled in the hills where God appeared through thick clouds and thunder. It's called Christ Pantokrator.

If you've seen Eastern icons before, you may have seen a picture of exactly this image. It's unsettling. Jesus is almost staring into your eyes, filling most of the frame. As you look at his face, you notice that the proportions are off. Staring squarely into his gaze, the icon resists symmetry in every facial feature. The right side is pristine and full of light while the left side traces shadow, wrinkle, and cracked skin. His eyes are different, and the nose is split right down the middle. Even his hair and beard alternate from left to right. This icon depicts the different sides of Jesus—the divine and the human—but it also invites us to see Jesus through different lenses and different vantage points, an essential practice for reading Revelation and much of the New Testament.

But even more, this word *pantokrator* may call us to see something deeper going on in Revelation. Like all good words, it has layers of meaning. Like the donkey from *Shrek* reminds us: Onions have layers. Ogres have layers. Words have layers. (Cakes have layers too.) God's pyrotechnics are everywhere in Revelation. Bowls of wrath, great battles, horsemen of the apocalypse, slaying a dragon, and scraping the stars from heaven. The images seem stolen straight out of the latest superhero summer blockbuster with multimillion-dollar special effects to boot. If you can hold your horsemen, we'll get to many of these in Chapters Five and Six, but first I need to highlight an undercurrent to this strange book—God is preserving and sustaining creation itself.

The word *pantokrator* is used only once in all of Paul's letters and never occurs in the Gospels. It is a favorite in Revelation, used nine times. *Pantokrator* is often translated as *almighty*. Whenever we got stuck in a discussion, my youth group always expected me, the kid who memorized all sorts of Bible verses and theological facts in school, to rattle off the "omnis" of God's character. God is omnipresent—all present or everywhere. God is omniscient—all knowing. God is omnipotent—all powerful. *Pantokrator* is often imagined as a description of God's power. God is almighty or all-powerful because of the description and characteristic that is outlined only in Revelation. For a word used so sparingly, it might surprise us to hear it so frequently in some the most treasured hymns of the church:

Holy, Holy, Holy, Lord God ***Almighty***,
Early in the morning, our song shall rise to thee.[22]

Praise to the Lord, ***the Almighty***, the King of Creation
O, my soul, praise him, for he is thy health and salvation.[23]

---

22 Reginald Heber. "Holy, Holy, Holy," *Evangelical Lutheran Worship, Pew Edition,* (Minneapolis, MN, Augsburg Fortress, 2006), #413.

23 Joachim Neander. "Praise to the Lord, the Almighty," *Evangelical Lutheran Worship, Pew Edition*, (Minneapolis, MN, Augsburg Fortress, 2006), #858.

Almighty's presence in our favorite hymns may have more to do with the fact that it appears in the Septuagint, the Greek translation of the Hebrew Bible. In some ways this is stating the obvious, but the Bible you might be reading on your table or off of your tablet is an exercise in translation. The New Testament (Revelation included) is written in Greek, the common language of commerce and learning in the ancient world. Jesus and the disciples likely spoke Aramaic, a language with deep connections to Hebrew. The Hebrew Bible is written in Hebrew, but many of the quotations found in the New Testament are made directly from the Greek translation of that Hebrew, the Septuagint. Before we get to our English translation, there is also a little pitstop through Latin, when Jerome translated the Bible into the Vulgate. From the year it was published in 382 and for more than twelve hundred years it was *the* translation of the Bible, until the work of Martin Luther who translated from the original Greek and Hebrew into the language of the people. And how does the Vulgate translate *pantokrator*? *Omnipotens.* Without a lick of Latin, I bet you can figure out what that means. *Omni* means all. *Potens* means potent or powerful. All-powerful. Our English word barely tweaks the spelling. The reformers encouraged translating the Bible into easily understandable language of the people, so many of our translations today work from the Hebrew and the Greek, but they are influenced by the theological pitstops through Greek and Latin.

Until nearly the age of ten, my daughter called the sea off the coast of California the "Specific Ocean." Because the ocean isn't my favorite, we've only been a few times. My daughter loves it, her little (big) specific ocean, the cold water and crashing waves she visits when we go to Nana and Papa's house in California. Now I get to give my own safety lecture every time we visit. I've resisted correcting the last remnants of their little-kid-ness because some part of me misses the fun repetition of phrases. I have to correct them now to avoid the meanness of other children (those little devils). But eventually, we come up with new ways to say words, new connections, new short-cuts, as language is always changing and adapting to the needs of the next generation. While I don't think we'll be seeing the Specific Ocean on maps anytime soon, I know just how much my own language has changed in my generation, let alone the language of a book painstakingly copied, translated, and shared for thousands of years. These words are layered, dense, fragile, uncertain, curious, and overflowing with meaning and possibility.

The word *pantokrator* that shows up consistently in Revelation is itself a translation of two concepts in the Hebrew Bible—*El Shaddai* and *YHWH Sabaoth*. The second name is the easiest and likely the strongest connection to God's power in Revelation. Sabaoth refers to the heavenly hosts, the angelic battalions that defend the heavens. God of the Heavenly Host is God who leads the angelic army in battle. While a somewhat foreign concept for us, this is a fairly consistent image of God in the Bible, where the people are always asking God to fight on their side. Revelation is full of hosts, angels, and battles. This tradition is certainly a part of *pantokrator*'s ubiquity in the text.

But the other Hebrew name is a little more interesting and tugs at us like the riptide, pulling us closer to the promise at the heart of this strange book. God is called *El Shaddai* only a few times, which I can't type without hearing Amy Grant singing it through my mom's cassette player. The word *Shaddai* shows up forty-eight times in all of the Hebrew Bible, only seven times as *El Shaddai*, *El* meaning God.[24] *Shaddai* is a bit of a mystery. The Greek and Latin translations insist that it must mean power, therefore translated as all-powerful *pantokrator* or *omnipotens*. But recent scholars think this is a pretty crude mistranslation. Rather, they suggest that *Shaddai* could mean wilderness or mountain, indicating God of the wilderness or God of

---

24 I've used numbers a couple of times to show you how important various words are in the Bible. It may seem a little arbitrary to just count the occurrences, but it gives us a sense of the variety of ways that the Bible uses language. To give you one point of reference, the name of God given to Moses, that practicing Jews substitute as The Name and our Bible translates as The Lord, occurs 6,828 times in the Hebrew Bible. Because *pantokrator* is such a special word, used only in Revelation and once in Paul's writing, we are looking for the unique characteristics that it shows us about God's work in and through Jesus Christ.

the mountain. *El Shaddai* may also refer to a feminine side to God's character, as mountains can also be a reference to breasts. That gives a whole new spin to Amy Grant's song, doesn't it? Just as a woman sustains a child with her body, God, the creator of all that is, sustains creation with intimacy, care, and love. Taking this one step further, *krator* could come from the Greek noun *kratos*, meaning strength or might. This is often imagined as military or empirical might—the strength of Rome demonstrated in the marching centurions or the economic power of wealth generated by the Pax Romana. Thus Christ is the conqueror, the victor of the great battle, who dominates the unconquerable Rome. But the definition of strength is also connected to the Greek verb *krateo*, meaning to hold or even sustain.[25]

Earlier in Revelation, Jesus *holds* the seven stars in his hand, using the same word tied to *pantokrator*. So perhaps, instead of a military head conquering the known universe, this image of God as *pantokrator* in Revelation is a vision of God *sustaining* all of creation. Reaching back to the beginning, to the creation story, this is a God who preserves the stuff of creation (plants, animals, humans, stars, sun, moon, seas, etc.) but also the *time* of creation. Often tied to the description of Jesus as *pantokrator*, all-sustainer is the repetition of the phrase, "who was and is and will forever be": "'I am the Alpha and the Omega,' says the Lord God, who is and who was and who is to come, the Almighty."[26]

This description of God's power shouldn't surprise us for how we meet Jesus in Revelation. The Jesus in Revelation is not a traveling rabbi spitting parables and healing the sick. Rather, we are meeting a Jesus who is waging battle on the side of those who have been trampled on the underside of history, beneath the wheels of empire. Jesus is calling forth a new order that returns to the vision that the

---

25 I'm showing a lot of my word-work here. Like the proofs they used to teach us in geometry class (ages ago!), I'm trying to shift our mental imagination and show you my homework. If you are interested in this topic and brave enough to read some radical theology/philosophy, take a look at John Caputo's book, *The Weakness of God: A Theology of the Event*. Buckle up, it's a trip.

26 Revelation 1:8

first verses of Scripture sing us toward. However, the world often defines victory as one people over and against another. Revelation articulates a radically different vision of victory in God's promise to sustain all that was, all that is, and all that will forever be. The way of Jesus in Revelation continues to be a way that defies traditional definitions of might-makes-right. Jesus doesn't win the celestial battle of good and evil because he is more powerful, has a stronger economic engine, or musters the most advanced weapons technology. In the upside-down logic of this way of love, Jesus continues to be the lamb who was slain, rather than transforming into an action superhero who will ride into battle and destroy all who stand in his way. Because the end of Revelation is the beginning, we can trust that God is creating something new in creation, not whisking away or demolishing the old world, but tending the creation that exists with love and care and redemption. When new things enter the world, however, the powers and structures that benefit from the status quo will rage, which is exactly where we're heading next.

6

A Hell of a Youth Event

We finally get into the fun stuff—hell, dragons, Satan, beasts, 666, the mark of the beast, and more. I will not be going through the entire book of Revelation to show you every strange corner of its vision. I'm skipping some really interesting and good stuff in order that you might be intrigued to dig a little deeper on your own. If you decide to dig, you'll find four horsemen of the apocalypse, bowls of wrath, trumpets, plagues, and so much more. The section of Revelation I've chosen is Revelation 12–13. I encourage you to read these two chapters, take some notes on your own, then come back and read my chapter. You've got some Bible swimming skills already (way to go!), so let's put them to the test in the deep end of Revelation's vast swimming pool. I promise the water wings will keep you afloat. Just remember Psalm 139: we can't go anywhere that God isn't—where God isn't whispering promise and beckoning good news. Read on, have courage, and trust that God is still doing a new thing because the end really is the beginning.

GREATEST CHRISTMAS PAGEANT EVER

I want you to imagine a Christmas pageant. You know the scene. Adorable, twinkly-eyed toddlers being shepherded by overwhelmed parents who barely got their clothes on in time to make it to church. As they line up for their costumes, you see some of the typical angels and hear some of the songs you would expect being rehearsed in the music room. When you look a little bit closer, however, some of the costuming looks a little bit off. The little cherubs put their pipe cleaner halos on and then move toward a rack of breastplates and swords, arming themselves for some kind of Christmas battle. Maybe it's a mashup of the Nutcracker this time? You chalk it up to the new youth minister, whose pageants seem to get more creative every year.

Alongside Grandma, Grandpa, and Aunt Marge, you find your seat in the sanctuary and wait for the kiddos to enter the stage. A prepubescent voice resounds from the loudspeaker, "A great portent appeared in heaven!"[1] Not exactly the opening that captured your imagination as your memory recalls the opening line, "And it came to pass in those days, that there went out a decree from Caesar Augustus that all the world should be taxed."[2] But, translations change, and so do Christmas pageants; you won't be a stick in the mud like your father always was. The lights come up to reveal a young lady clothed in a sparkling gown with a long iridescent cape glittering from the twinkle lights sewn all over it. She's standing on a giant papier-mache globe that is either a wheel of cheese or the moon. No opening song, just a scream and cry issuing from the girl who appears to be in pain.

Before someone can get up to see if anything is wrong with her, the voice speaks again from the loudspeaker, this time like some announcer for a wrestling match: "Another portent appeared in heaven."[3] Prowling slowly from the back of the room, eight fifth-grade boys duck under a bed sheet covered in long strips of red and

---

1 Revelation 12:1
2 Luke 2:1, KJV
3 Revelation 12:3

orange crepe paper with a surprisingly tall sixth-grader leading the way as the head of a dragon. The dragon's tail swings with a few giggles from the fifth-grade rear section and disturbs the first-grade section dressed beautifully as golden stars. A third of them scatter, running toward the families looking on and singing a dissonant song, "Starlight, star-bright, first star I see tonight . . ." Grandma elbows you in the ribs, "What kind of Christmas pageant *is* this?"

The action stops abruptly as all of the children sing the beloved, if somewhat obscure, Christmas hymn:

> Of the Father's love begotten,
> ere the worlds began to be,
> He is Alpha and Omega,
> He the Source, the Ending He,
> of the things that are, that have been,
> and that future years shall see
> evermore and evermore![4]

Grandma seems to settle in a bit more as the baby is born and the woman with the golden sequined dress holds a doll tenderly in her arms. But the music starts to turn a little more dissonant as the pipe organ enters and the adult choir sings the third verse from behind a curtain:

> . . . pow'rs, dominions, bow before Him
> and extol our God and King;
> let no tongue on earth be silent,
> every voice in concert ring,
> evermore and evermore!

The sixth-grade head of the dragon pulls the greatest pyrotechnic feat you've seen in church. It opens its mouth and glitter flies in the

---

4 Marcus Aurelius Clemens Prudentius. "Of the Father's Love Begotten," *Evangelical Lutheran Worship, Pew Edition*, (Minneapolis, MN, Augsburg Fortress, 2006), #294).

air as you hear distinctly from behind, "I wonder who's going to clean that up." Now marching to the beat, the dragon gets closer and closer to the woman, clearly trying to devour the child. But, just as the glitter monster opens its maw, the worship band comes in with a 1980s hair band anthem sung by one of your favorite children of the congregation. I mean there's no such thing as "favorite children," but of course there is. The music director's daughter always sings a stunning solo in nearly every choral anthem, and you heard the other day that she is thinking about going to college for musical theater. Michaela is dressed in what might be a leftover Captain America costume from Halloween but spray-painted gold and covered in glitter. She has golden make-up on her face and she is leading an army of toddlers, half of whom are jousting each other with foam swords and the other half are ambling aimlessly behind Michaela as she sings the ongoing hook to the song, "Worthy is the lamb that was slain!" and drives her sword into the heart of the dragon, who giggles once more before the train of crepe paper slowly deflates to the ground. The adult choir once more sings from behind the curtain:

Rejoice then, you heavens
and those who dwell in them!
But woe to the earth and the sea,
for the devil has come down to you
with great wrath
because he knows that his time is short![5]

While you are distracted by the action with the dragon, you miss that somehow the baby-doll is tied to monofilament line and floating toward the ceiling. The woman at center stage unclips her sparkling cape and runs toward stage left where a lone cactus stands with a brown cardboard sign that reads in elementary blue marker, "Wilderness."

---

5 Revelation 12:10

The lights come up, and the crowd is restless. Unsure whether to applaud or laugh or riot, families slowly start to clap, looking nervously at one another. The pastor stands up, looking equally baffled, and says, "Thank you to the entire team who worked tirelessly to produce this year's Christmas pageant. It certainly will be a moment none of us will forget." The tension in the room relieves into nervous laughter as you finally look more closely at the program handed to you by an eager youth at the door: "A Great Portent: The Christmas Story through the Book of Revelation."

Who said Revelation isn't for kids? I've been shopping around for a church that will take me up on my offer to write a Christmas pageant through the most obscure Christmas narrative of the Bible. Of course we imagine Luke's version, the time when Quirinus was governor of Syria, the shepherds and angels, the stable and manger, the ox and . . . donkey (it's for the kids!). Or, we might turn to Matthew's distinctive Christmas account. It opens with a long genealogy, a list of the families of the Hebrew Scriptures that lead up to Jesus's birth; it doesn't give Mary nearly enough lines and includes the holy family's early escape to Egypt alongside Herod's infamous slaughter of the innocents. The other two gospels, Mark and John, don't open with a birth narrative at all. Mark gets right into the action at Jesus's baptism by John the Baptist. John opens with a poem that sounds more like the story of creation than the birth of a child. The only other story in the Bible of the birth of Jesus, the child who would change the world, comes in Revelation chapter twelve. I've recounted it creatively as a Christmas pageant, but take a few minutes to read the verses of chapter twelve yourself.

This chapter is the perfect entry point for our final plunge into Revelation. We'll be walking through some of the scarier images that Revelation uses, connecting them to their context in the early moments of the Jesus movement, then pondering how they unveil monsters that might be lurking in our own backyards. To be clear, I'm not advocating to switch our readings at Christmas every year to Revelation. My email and voicemail would be overflowing, and I'm sure I'd see an angrier mob than Stravinsky's premier of *Rite of*

Spring.[6] However, I have taught bits of this story at Christmastime because it highlights the ways that multiple voices can tell a much broader story of what is going on. The Gospel of John's poem reaches all the way to the beginning, framing the coming of Jesus in much the same way as Revelation—the end is the beginning. Matthew's genealogy connects the birth of Jesus with the generational longing of the Jewish people, including naming a number of women whose surprising presence in this ancient list quietly contradicts many of the misogynistic tendencies of Christian practice throughout the centuries.

Revelation's Christmas narrative broadens the scope of the birth of Jesus, who is the child born to the woman crying out in pain. It places the birth of this child as a cosmic threat to powers that rebel against God, namely the dragon. Revelation is perfectly clear who the dragon in the narrative is: "The great dragon was thrown down, that ancient serpent, who is called the devil and Satan, the deceiver of the whole world—he was thrown down to the earth, and his angels were thrown down with him."[7] But wait, I thought the serpent wasn't Satan? I promise, we'll get to Satan in the next chapter, but first a little pitstop in hell. Come along! It will be surprising—and fun, in the way that a Revelation Christmas pageant is fun.

A HELL OF A YOUTH EVENT

My friend Derek loves ice fishing. It's a favorite activity in the freezing climate where I live. One winter he offered to take me out on the

---

6 My spouse said I'm allowed exactly one classical music nerd reference in this book. So here it is. In 1913, Igor Stravinsky premiered a new ballet called *The Rite of Spring*. The piece has been cited as one of the most influential in the twentieth century, shaping vision for modernist music for nearly a century to come. But the people who experienced that first gathering—well, they rioted, or so the legend has it. If you want to read more, the BBC has a nice little article on it from 2013: Ivan Hewitt, May 29, 2013, "Did The Rite of Spring Really Spark a Riot?" BBC News, https://www.bbc.com/news/magazine-22691267

7 Revelation 12:9

frozen lake near his house. I hopped on the back of his small snowmobile and off we went, towing a drill, a small heater, a pull-over shelter, and a few beers. I smuggled Swedish fish in my pocket because I can't really go anywhere without some form of gummy candy. Derek grew up in a fairly conservative Lutheran megachurch surrounded by even more conservative Evangelical churches in Fargo, North Dakota. Don't worry; he gets me nowhere near a wood-chipper. Derek went to parochial school, loved video games and *Star Wars*, and grew up in the 1990s and early oughts. As you can imagine, our childhoods have a lot of overlap even though we grew up in wildly different geographies, so a frequent topic of conversation is our upbringing. For those of us whose faith has evolved somewhat, it feels a bit like an ongoing community to bump into people who have grown in ways, who are also still searching for answers to the questions that they grew up with. Derek is far more Lutheran than I am, but I don't hold that against him.

One of my favorite stories from Derek's childhood is when he was invited by one of the more conservative Baptist churches in town to attend a simulation of hell. I've seen a lot in my time living in Evangelical circles. I've heard speaking in tongues, seen (deeply traumatizing) "documentaries" scaring teens away from abortion, and tried (more than once) to *Kiss Dating Goodbye*. I have never—I *had* never heard about a simulation of hell. Apparently the building was arranged in concentric circles, which fascinated me from the start. Why would they model their hell off Dante's *Inferno*? I guess because the Bible doesn't have a whole lot to say about this place where the evil go after they die, but we'll get into that shortly. Each room offered an invitation to turn back, showing how the results of sin were nothing fun or glorious at all. At the center of the circle, the head pastor of the Baptist church worked the teens into a fury, preaching about the damnation that awaited all of them if they did not repent of their sin and turn to Jesus. Two high school girls were chained to the pastor (ick!), saying that they got there by smoking weed. The pastor played the part of Satan, professing that in hell drinking and sex were ever present, happening twenty-four hours a day. At the center of the circle, Derek, the cheeky high school kid from the Lutheran church across town stood up and said to the pastor: "That sounds great! How do I get there again?"

Hell is a core part of contemporary imagination for Christians. Heaven is where we want to end up. Hell is what we want to avoid. Not quite as many as believe in heaven (71 percent), but 58 percent of Americans believe in hell.[8] True confession here, I swear a little. My kids know words are bad largely because they're words "daddy uses." The other day I must have said something about hell in an off-handed way. My girls caught me right away, "Daddy! You said a bad word!" In that moment I realized that my girls have no understanding of this place of torment that occupied so much of my imagination as a child. Connected directly to the "rapture anxiety" we explored in the last chapter is the fear of life in eternal torment.

Most of our ideas of hell, however, come from nowhere in the Bible. Again, I'm rearranging lots of mental furniture for those of us who grew up in fundamentalism. We were brought up to trust the doctrine that had been passed along to us about heaven, hell, predestination, the rapture, and many more quagmires of theology. Further, we were taught that these doctrines came from God, written right in the pages of the Bible. I've found that it is exceedingly helpful to show people where our ideas of hell come from, so in the following sections I present to you a brief history of hell.[9]

SHEOL—HEBREW SCRIPTURE'S PIT

The Hebrew Scriptures do not have a singular vision of hell as a place of perpetual torment. The afterlife is not a major theme of Jewish

---

8 Pew Research, "Views on the afterlife: Majorities of U.S. adults say they believe in heaven, hell," November 23, 2021, https://www.pewresearch.org /religion/2021/11/23/views-on-the-afterlife/

9 This is by no means exhaustive. If you are curious about the development of these ideas over the centuries, I encourage you to read Bart Ehrman's *Heaven & Hell: A History of the Afterlife* (New York: Simon & Schuster, 2020).

spirituality or the witness we have in the longest pages of the Bible. The closest we get is a Hebrew word, *Sheol*, which literally means the pit. Recalling a passage from the key I shared at the very beginning of this book (the end truly is the beginning!):

> Where can I go from your spirit?
> Or where can I flee from your presence?
> If I ascend to heaven, you are there;
> if I make my bed in Sheol, you are there.[10]

Many ancients believed in the cutting-edge science of their day, that the earth was part of a three-tiered universe. In Genesis 1, God stretches space between the waters, creating what the King James Version translates as a firmament, a sort of membrane that keeps the chaotic waters before creation at bay so that God can do a new thing on the earth. The earth is in the center of this three-tier universe. On the top are the heavens, where the throne room of God sits, looking out "across the glassy sea."[11] From an ancient perspective, it makes a lot of sense. Why would the sky be blue like the sea if not for the fact that water lived above the membrane (firmament) of the heavens? Water falls from heavens in rain because of the glassy sea above the earth. Then we all live in the middle space, like Tolkien's Middle Earth. And below, beneath the firmament at the bottom of creation is the pit, the furthest place from God's heavenly throne room. It is the place where humans go when they die; thus our key that we can't flee from God's love in any state of being, heaven-bent or earthbound, full of life or in the throes of the grave. In the Hebrew Bible's understanding of Sheol, this is the grave where humans go when they die. It isn't a place of perpetual torment, simply a hole in the ground where dead people live. Scary? Sure, dead people are scary. But it doesn't scream with torture or monsters. And the Hebrew Bible isn't interested in keeping people out of this place. It is inevitable. We all go there.

---

10 Psalm 139:7–8
11 Reginald Helber, "Holy, Holy, Holy," 1826.

JESUS GETS APOCALYPTIC

My mother-in-law often wants me to help her find a way out of some of the challenging corners of Scripture. She is a deeply faithful woman, but the more she reads the Bible, the more troubled she becomes. A mother of queer children, she has big bones to pick with the few passages used to clobber the folks she loves dearly. When I list them all for her (because I've argued these for too long to not have them on the tip of my tongue), she writes off all the Old Testament verses because when Jesus came that old stuff doesn't matter. When I list the passages in Paul's letters, she always pokes holes in Paul: "What did he know? He didn't meet Jesus!" Of course he did, after he had risen on the road to Damascus, but that isn't the point. She wants most of all to know what came from Jesus's mouth on the matter. Which, according to the gospels, is exactly zilch.

Finding the exact words that came from Jesus's mouth is a real challenge. Rather, we have fragments of sayings, stories passed a generation later, bits that Paul shared that he heard from apostles like Peter, and the testimonies of the gospels that were compiled a couple generations later. We don't have access to the words of Jesus on the topic of homosexuality nor (entirely) on the topic of hell. I assure my mother-in-law that the gospels share an image of Jesus who is far more concerned with what we do with our money than who we love and marry and build families with. She likes this line and thinks about bringing it to the next sticky conversation with someone who thinks quite differently in conservative central Minnesota. For the founder of a religion that is so often heaven-bent or hell-avoidant, Jesus doesn't have a lot to say about the subject. Even though my mother-in-law would like to know exactly which bits of the New Testament came from Jesus's mouth and which bits might have been apostles taking liberties with the message, we are left with only the texts in front of us. And Jesus has some apocalyptic fire to share. Jesus's apocalyptic sermons and stories are the sections of Scripture that a mainline preacher might gloss over, skip, or avoid.

Some of these passages also may have been fiercely preached if you grew up in a tradition that tends toward brimstone.

In one such passage (Matthew 25:3–46) most often cited by progressive Christians to display Jesus's preferential option for the poor,[12] Jesus also has some fiery words for the people who did not take care of the hungry, thirsty, naked, sick, or imprisoned. Jesus is speaking in a parable about a day of judgment, when the Son of Man will come in glory with the angels to separate the sheep from the goats—the sheep on the right hand, who had cared for "even the least of these," and the goats on the left hand who had not: "And these will go away into eternal punishment but the righteous into eternal life."[13] Jesus sends away those he calls accursed, who ignored the suffering among them, into "the eternal fire prepared for the devil and his angels."[14] Reading from this side of our contemporary imagination of heaven and hell, Jesus seems very clear. The sheep are welcomed into the kingdom of heaven and the goats are sent to hell, where there is eternal fire, the devil, and his angels. It's clear which side of the line we want to be on. But, looking a bit more closely, "it is the fire that is eternal, not the sinner in the fire. The fires never go out. Just as the funeral pyre burns on once the body is consumed—or, more appropriately, just as the executioner's fire continues to burn after the condemned has

---

12 A "preferential option for the poor" is a fairly common phrase in social justice and progressive Christian circles today. It refers to a movement that began among liberation theologians, largely in Latin America. Father Gustavo Gutiérrez was one of the first to articulate the way that Scripture articulates God's ongoing work on behalf of the poor and marginalized. Passages in the Hebrew Bible offer specific concern and care for the poor, the widow, the orphan, and the immigrant. Jesus's teaching and miracles have overwhelming concern for those on the margins of society, and of course Matthew 25 is a common reference point for this teaching. This impulse has influenced Evangelical, Roman Catholic, and mainline communities across the United States. As someone coming out of American Evangelicalism, I first came into contact with this theme in Shane Claiborne's book, *The Irresistible Revolution*.

13 Matthew 25:46

14 Matthew 25:41

long since died—so too with the fires of eternal punishment. Like the worm that never dies, it goes on, but the people who are punished have expired. They will no longer exist."[15]

Jesus's images are more commonplace than transcendent. He's talking about a good offering and a bad offering, a sheep and a goat. This parable envisions a kingdom that Jesus is beckoning forth, already and not yet. When he points to those who are not acting in alignment with the new vision, the response is destruction, not perpetual torture. Jesus also uses a specific historical location that could have instilled more fear than fire—burial without care, in the most undesirable place outside Jerusalem: Gehenna.

In an extended sermon decrying "woe" against religious insiders, Jesus repeatedly connects their actions with Gehenna, which even today is translated as "hell" in the New Revised Standard Version. Gehenna, however, is a physical place outside of Jerusalem, a valley that lies outside the city walls. Some scholars have proposed that it was a garbage heap with fires that were constantly burning from all of the refuse (thus eternal fires). Other scholars have suggested that this was a place of human sacrifice to gods opposed to the God of Israel. Either way, Jesus is saying that these folks will have the worst fate of all—a burial in a place that has been ritually desecrated or flooded with filthy refuse, the place furthest from God's presence in the temple just up the hill in Jerusalem.[16] So, for my mother in law, and for any of you who want to know, Jesus wasn't describing a place of perpetual torment in the gospels. He wasn't articulating an existential place where souls will go after they die. Jesus was describing what happens when people ignore the poor among us

---

15 Bart Ehrman, *Heaven and Hell: A History of the Afterlife* (New York: Simon & Schuster, 2020), 165–166.

16 Ehrman, 157–158. For those who notice, I am not including an exhaustive history that would include Paul's views and all the gospel writers. This is more of a sample platter of early Christian views. For a more exhaustive examination, read both Ehrman's book mentioned here and some of Amy Jill Levine's work, such as *The Difficult Words of Jesus* (Nashville: Abingdon, 2021).

or allow religious posturing to exclude people in our midst rather than prescribing eternal punishment for people who are not on the right side of the sorting line.

REVELATION'S LAKE OF FIRE

I'm too young (and too eager) for grunge music. I much prefer the hopped-up anthems of pop-punk music, which my youngest gladly bounces to in the backseat when I am feeling nostalgic for my youth. But here goes a reference to grunge, just because it feels like it might be the best tone for Revelation's innovation of hell. The late lead singer of Nirvana, Kurt Cobain, sang Scripture for MTV's *Unplugged*, some of my favorite recordings of all time. A very different vision than the teens gathered in the opening scenes of *A Thief in the Night*, MTV filmed a small stage of the great teen bands for an acoustic concert of their favorite songs. The song entitled "Lake of Fire" asks the eternal question, "Where do bad folks go when they die?" and responds with the most creative rhymes of hellfire that I've ever heard, pairing the verb "fry" with "fourth of Ju-ly." Some of the most fearsome passages in Revelation have to do with a seemingly perpetual torment in a lake of fire. Far before Cobain's performance, Jonathan Edwards conjured the image of endless torment to frighten Puritans into faith in some of the earliest words of American literature:

> Unconverted men walk over the pit of hell on a rotten covering, and there are innumerable places in this covering so weak that they will not bear their weight, and these places are not seen . . . they have deserved the fiery pit, and are already sentenced to it; and God is dreadfully provoked, his anger is as great towards them as to those that are actually suffering the executions of the fierceness of his wrath in hell, and they have done nothing in the least to appease or abate that anger, neither is God in the least bound by any promise to hold them up one moment; the

devil is waiting for them, hell is gaping for them, the flames gather and flash about them, and would fain lay hold on them, and swallow them up.[17]

This fiery imagination was flamed even further in a film of my childhood—Disney's *The Hunchback of Notre Dame*. In Stephen Schwartz and Alan Menken's haunting anthem, "Hellfire," a judge wrestles with his desire for Esmerelda, blaming her for his lust. His notes reek of racism and evil, while Frollo prays to Maria, the Virgin Mary, for guidance even as he turns toward hatred. Fires lick the screen and terrified me as a kid, even as I didn't understand the way the fire revealed the hatred of the overzealous, misogynistic faithful.

Revelation does not articulate a vision of hell like any one of these examples. Perhaps this has become a recurring theme, but our imagination of hell is formed much later. The more familiar images are drawn from a single passage in Revelation that envisions the torment for Babylon, which represents Rome and all its oppression. The nation that had once destroyed the temple in Jerusalem and sent the people of Israel into exile is a direct analogy to the current occupying army. Now fallen, Revelation sees the consequences of their actions falling in upon itself: "they will also drink the wine of God's wrath, poured unmixed into the cup of his anger, and they will be tormented with fire and sulfur in the presence of the holy angels and in the presence of the Lamb. And the smoke of their torment goes up forever and ever. There is no rest day or night for those who worship the beast and its image and for anyone who receives the brand of its name."[18]

To our ears that are tuned with Frollo's damning solo and Edwards's sermon bursting with brimstone, this verse from Revelation sounds exactly like the vision of hell that attempted to scare salvation into teenagers in Fargo. But, once again, the context is everything. Revelation contrasts the perpetual *rest* of the martyrs with the *unrest*

---

17 Jonathan Edwards, "Sinners in the Hands of an Angry God," 1741.
18 Revelation 14:10–11

experienced in the torment of their occupying force. For a people living under the thumb of an unwanted oppressor who had recently destroyed the temple that held all of their practice and experience of God's love and goodness, these words would hold hope. The violence of the ruling authority would be its own destruction, and God would sustain and preserve the witnesses, those who may have felt like following Christ was an impossible decision. The direct opposite of Revelation's end, where there is no day or night because God is the light of all creation, the destruction of Babylon says there is "no rest" day or night. There is no sabbath—no basking in God's holiness—because this empire made its choice. Further, even though the verse says their torment will be eternal, Revelation itself does not support this. At the end of Revelation, just before the beautiful visions we've been tracing at the end of the book, in chapter nineteen all of the violent representatives of empire are destroyed completely, not held in torment forever.

While Revelation mentions martyrs for faith in the opening letters with their honored place at God's altar, persecution (or prosecution, more accurately[19]) worsened in the centuries that followed. Revelation redefines victory through apocalyptic imagination. As Dr. Brueggemann writes, "the Book of Revelation is neither 'otherworldly' escapism nor is it about life after death. It is rather an act of insistent imagination that competes with and resists the imposing world of Rome."[20] The Roman world enforced victory through empirical might—political, economic, and military. Revelation offers a radical and offensive alternative to Rome's definition of victory in

---

19 This is decidedly a rabbit hole, so I will leave you with a brief note here. Shifting many of the inherited narratives of preachers and Christians, Candida Moss "reveals that the 'Age of Martyrs' is a fiction—there was no sustained three-hundred-year-long effort by the Romans to persecute Christians. While there were some martyrs, most of these stories were pious exaggerations and even forgeries designed to marginalize heretics, inspire the faithful, and fund churches." Candida Moss, *The Myth of Persecution: How Early Christians Invented a Story of Martyrdom* (New York: Harper One, 2013).

20 Walter Brueggemann, *Church Anew*, July 19, 2023.

Jesus Christ, the lamb who was slain, whose power is in weakness, whose wisdom is scandal, and who will sustain this world through any power that tries to dominate it.[21]

So how do we get from a pit, a grave, a garbage pile, and a fire to a vision of hell as a place of perpetual torment and torture? My spouse's late grandfather was one of my favorite souls on earth. At Christmastime he would look for the King James Bible to read the Christmas story because the modern translations were insufficient. But where the KJV rings with poetry and nostalgia, it includes more than a few mistranslations. While it can't hold the entire blame, the good old King James Version translates each of our plot points on this brief history of hell in a way that misses the original meaning and spins a specific theological vision. Sheol becomes hell. Gehenna becomes hell. Hades becomes hell. Translations can have painful consequences but power may have more to do with the recipe of hell we see today.

There were various moments of persecution of Christians in the centuries that follow Revelation, as the Christian message spreads and the dynamics of power shift. In a great reversal of history and of the religious tradition, Constantine, the Roman Emperor, converts to Christianity and issues the Edict of Milan in 313, where Christianity becomes the official religion of the empire. After the edict, Christianity is transformed into a force on the world's stage throughout decisive moments of history. A result of Christianity's role in power is that hell could become a tool to enforce orthodoxy, to define who is part of the public life, and to actively exclude, harm, persecute, or even kill people. When I joked about hell in the back of a youth group van, it belied a real fear that was ever present in my experience of church growing up, as perhaps it was for you. Hell was the threat of walking down the wrong pathway, a narrow trail marked by moral policing, enforced by purity culture, and carrying

---

21 Barbara Rossing's marvelous book helped me see the way that victory (in Revelation often the word translated *conquered* or *conquerors* can be rendered as *victor, victory,* or *victorious*. Rossing, 103–108.

the weight of shame. Growing up under this mantle can result in a clear sense of fear and significant mental health concerns. Suicide risk among LGBTQ+ Christian teens, for example, is doubled for those whose parents oppose homosexuality. For teens whose parents do not espouse negative connections of religion and LGBTQ identity, religion can actually reduce rates of suicide attempts.[22] The specter of hell associated with emerging sexual orientation or gender identity can induce terror and fear and trauma. When hell is a tool wielded by the powerful, it enforces morality in ways that perpetuate exclusion and harm. But in the original context, the lake of fire and the absence of rest meant that the powerful would receive justice for all the harm that they had inflicted. Revelation was originally balm for a people who were living under the consistent weight of empire's demands. Like many of the vantage points in Revelation, it depends on which side of the line you stand on. And the powerful have wielded hell throughout Christian history.

The Hunchback of Notre Dame points at a much deeper evil than the sexual desire of a twisted official. Threats of damnation resulted in torture and execution in the inquisition, witch trials that murdered tens of thousands of women in Europe and the colonies, horrors of the crusades, and countless atrocities across the centuries. As Christianity became an empire, it lost the core message of a book like Revelation that once provided hope, promise, possibility, and imagination to a fledgling Christian community. The church across the ages, and in some expressions still today, fell on the wrong side of the line that Revelation draws in the sand. In its strange imagery and fiery visions, the destruction of the forces of empire serves as a warning for a church that at times has traded its authentic witness for power and placement. Empire is not victorious, and its violence is ultimately self-destructive. Power is found instead in the voice of the lamb who was slain. How we read Revelation matters. And if we

---

22 "Religiosity and Suicidality Among LGBTQ Youth," *The Trevor Project*, April 14, 2020, https://www.thetrevorproject.org/research-briefs/religiosity-and -suicidality-among-lgbtq-youth/

simply ignore it, others will fill the void with interpretations that make the same mistakes as generations previously. We need not look to ancient history to find the true evil in Frollo's fiery solo. For me, I need only look at my congregation and look in the mirror.

CONFIRMED. RADICALIZED.

A young man was confirmed in a Lutheran church of the same denomination that I serve. According to his pastor, he attended church services regularly with his family, went to church camp, and was a student in confirmation classes not unlike the hundreds of young white men that I have taught in our suburban Lutheran congregation of the Evangelical Lutheran Church in America. After dropping out of high school in ninth grade, tending a drug habit, and living in online isolation, the young man was twenty-one years old. Radicalized by online corners of hatred and bigotry, on June 17, 2015, he entered the Mother Emmanuel AME Church in Charleston, South Carolina, a historic Black congregation. He sat in Bible study with this community of Christians for one hour before he opened fire, killing nine people in a hate-filled rampage.[23] In the sentencing hearing, "Felicia Sanders, one of the few survivors [of the shooting], told the courtroom early on that [he] belonged in the pit of hell. Months later, she said that because of him she can no longer close her eyes to pray. She can't stand to hear the sound of firecrackers, or even the patter of acorns falling."[24]

---

23 I choose not to name the man who currently sits on death row for the thirty-three counts for which he was convicted. I will, however, name the nine lives that were ended in his hate-filled rampage: the Rev. Clementa Pinckney, Cynthia Hurd, the Rev. Sharonda Coleman-Singleton, Tywanza Sanders, Ethel Lance, Susie Jackson, Rev. Depayne Middleton-Doctor, the Rev. Daniel Simmons, and Myra Thompson.

24 Rachel Kaadzi Ghansah, August 21, 2017, *GQ*, "A Most American Terrorist: The Making of Dylann Roof," https://www.gq.com/story/dylann-roof-making-of-an-american-terrorist

The pit of hell and the fires of Revelation seem a fitting ending to evil such as this, but it is also the beginning. The Southern Poverty Law Center (SPLC) chronicles the beliefs of countless hate groups, carefully studying their activities, motivations, publications, and memberships to expose them to the public, media, and law enforcement. They work tirelessly to chronicle the tactics of white supremacist groups which, like the ideology that motivated the killer described previously, draw from religious imagery, twisting it toward hateful ends. More specifically, images from Scripture, and more mainstream Evangelical interpretations of Revelation, become source material for such groups: "Religious concepts—such as Christian end times prophecy, millennialism and the belief that the Second Coming of Jesus Christ is imminent—play a vital role in the recruitment, radicalization and mobilization of violent right-wing extremists and their illegal activities in the United States."[25] We don't know whether the murderer knew or read the Book of Revelation, but the internet is full of pathways toward radicalization, where lonely white men find far too many sources of hatred. Google searches, YouTube, TikTok, social media sites, and online message boards become a covert community for white supremacists or white Christian nationalists to find leaders and narratives that embolden their radicalization and reveal alternative ideologies that further twist the message of Revelation. Many of the participants in the January 6 attack on the US Capitol, for example, were members of various militia groups, described again by the SPLC by their adherence to particular interpretations of Revelation:

some militia members believe that the so-called "Anti-Christ" in the last days predicted in the Book of Revelation is a world leader that unites all nations under a "one world government" before being exposed as the agent of Satan. They further believe that Jesus will battle the Anti-Christ before restoring his

---

25 Daryl Johnson, *The Intelligence Report,* "Holy Hate: The Far-Right's Radicalization of Religion" (Montgomery: Southern Poverty Law Center, Spring 2018).

kingdom on earth. Militia members cite the creation of Communism, the establishment of the United Nations, and attacks against their Constitutional rights as "signs" or "evidence" that the Anti-Christ is actively working to create the "one world government" predicted in the Bible (e.g. Book of Revelation).[26]

It is essential to refute these false claims of Revelation and these perversions of the faith expressed throughout the witness of Scripture. Anti-Christ, as we have already discussed, does not appear in Revelation, rather is an interpretation of 1 Thessalonians 2:3, where a "lawless one" or "man of sin" becomes a specific character in the drama of rapture theology and popularized by *Left Behind*. Like the Q-Anon fears of global elite, only a very sideways, ill-informed, and scantily Scriptured interpretation of Revelation could provide back-up for a "one world government." Xenophobia and nationalism stoke a fear of international cooperation, thus influencing a complicated interpretation of a variety of texts in the Bible.[27] It takes speculative leaps that wildly depart from Scripture to arrive at this outlook, but the gap is narrowed by the popularization of rapture theology in popular culture and in the pulpit.

Even more frightening, the killer at Mother Emmanuel church professed a desire to start a "race war," a belief that unites a growing number of the so-called alt-right:

> They are young, they are white, and they often brag about their arsenals of guns, because these are the guns that will save them in the coming race war. They are armed to the teeth, and almost always, they are painfully undereducated or somewhat educated but extremely socially awkward. That is, until their eyes are opened to the fact that within the world of white supremacy

---

26 Daryl Johnson.

27 I can't walk through the vast network of interpretive leaps, but Barbara Rossing does an incredible job of this in *The Rapture Exposed: The Message of Hope in the Book of Revelation*.

they can find friends. What once alienated them now helps them relate to others, people like [the Mother Emmanuel shooter], over a common desire to start a race war.[28]

To be crystal clear, Revelation is not a book that justifies war of any sort. But for a hate group on the lookout for texts to justify their aims at violence, to enflame their embattled sense of identity, or to even find gifts in martyrdom, Revelation can provide source material in the Bible itself. How we read Revelation matters. How we envision hell matters. It has life-and-death consequences. For those of us who teach Scripture, if we leave it alone or chalk it up to only the wingnuts, we are derelict in our duty. And we ultimately leave the work of interpretation up to those who might misuse, twist, and radicalize its messages. The great battles in Revelation 12–20 are filled with images that can be subtly twisted into a narrative that confirms ideologies of hatred. Looking for proof texts to acts of hatred, Revelation can look like a roadmap for war. For isolated white men who feel embattled by the changing culture, they may begin to see a frontline to take up arms. The strange numbers in Revelation can become a code to predict or analyze events in daily life. Even the murderer looked to numbers to find meaning and purpose: "he went to a local library and used the computer there to create a Facebook account. He added 88 'friends,' and the majority of them were black kids who went to high school with him. Eighty-eight because *H* is the eighth letter of the alphabet and two *H'*s is Nazi shorthand for 'Heil Hitler.'"[29] But the numbers in Revelation, as we have already discussed, are a lot easier to understand and provide hope to those on the margins, not backup to hateful ideologies. Likewise, the beasts of Revelation are not intended to provide weapons for hatred but undermine the powers of this world and their complicity in acts of violence and systems of oppression.

---

28 Ghanash.
29 Ghanash.

As I look out on the young white men in confirmation classes, I feel an increasing responsibility to *reveal* the stranger passages of Scripture for them. The line has faded between fringe conspiracy theories and mainstream theological interpretations. If Revelation continues to be a part of our null curriculum, untouched and unacknowledged, we risk ceding all interpretive ground to those who might wield hell and rapture and numbers and more for hatred. But if we lean into the intrigue, move toward the mystique, perhaps we can invite young people to hear the hope that is calling out of these pages. If we can invite people into conversation about this text, wondering which side of the line of power they often sit on, perhaps they might hear the words of judgment, challenge, or conviction more clearly. There are indeed monsters lurking in these corners of Revelation, but they don't need to scare us. There are monsters enough in our midst for that.

I may not be bold enough to debut the Great Portent Christmas Pageant in our sanctuary just yet. But I can recall clearly the twinkling faces of kids as I described the Christmas story they'd never heard of. Dressed in Christmas best, a few children doodled on paper while I preached the Christmas Eve sermon. They knew the story and the rhythm of worship. They knew when to tune out to the drone of the preacher. I mentioned all the favorite characters—shepherds, angels, sheep, Mary and Joseph, a donkey, and an innkeeper. We sang the favorite carols and basked in the evening candlelight. But when I mentioned dragons? Their ears perked up. When I talked about scraping stars from the heavens? They got curious. There is something startling about hearing anew the story that we think we know so well. Jesus is born for a season when monsters are prowling, not below beds or on late-night TV, but in our communities and on our national broadcasts. Amid the "Silent Night" and "All Is Calm," it is easy to get lulled into a predictability of the story. But the threat was and is real. A dragon prowls, ready to devour the child who might change the world. While we mark our sanctuaries with crosses, the public execution of Jesus by the Roman Empire was a complete embarrassment for those who "proclaim Christ crucified, a stumbling block to Jews and foolishness to gentiles."[30] The scandal of the cross reveals the kind of victory that the Lamb sustains throughout Revelation. It is a victory that overturns expectations of power and might, that reverses empire's economics, and that reveals a way of wholeness for all of creation.

Eventually the dragon is defeated by God's heavenly army, who stands up for the faithful, the martyrs, the witnesses to good news. The justice received by the dragon is empire's own doing, while the victory of the Lamb inverts power and preserves all of creation. "They have conquered him by the blood of the Lamb and by the word of their testimony."[31] The songs in heaven continue, the ongoing worship draws the story back into focus, ever beating the drum that we are formed for an alternative community, alternative allegiance, alternative economy, and alternative victory in the practice of liturgy. While we await the best Christmas pageant ever, perhaps we will have to make do with the moody and ancient Christmas hymn, drawn right from the pages of Revelation:

> O ye heights of heaven adore Him;
> Angel hosts, His praises sing;
> Powers, dominions, bow before Him,
> and extol our God and King!
> Let no tongue on earth be silent,
> Every voice in concert sing,
> Evermore and evermore![32]

God's promise is forever. It cannot be broken, and it cannot be tempered by threats of hell or protestations of the powerful. Let us sing our children, our youth, our elders, the vulnerable, and the privileged. As we sing the hymns that can form our imagination together, may we all be drawn into the heavenly worship "evermore and evermore"!

---

30 1 Corinthians 1:23

31 Revelation 12:11

32 Marcus Aurelius Clemens Prudentius, "Of the Father's Love Begotten," tr. composite, ELW 295.

7

Route 666 to Rome and Beyond

We end our time together reading the great confrontation with Satan, listening to the way that the identity of the devil has developed over the centuries. Take some time to read Revelation 16–18 carefully, using all the skills that we've built together. By now, you'll see clearly that real forces are operating throughout Revelation. Rather than spiritualizing the beasts, we will confront the systems and empires that operate in opposition to the sustaining, life-giving power of God and the Lamb.

666 AND ROME'S BEASTS

I was never prouder than when my eldest told me her ultimate favorite fast food—Wendy's chicken nuggets. While it always presented a challenge because our youngest preferred the golden arches (parents of young kids, you know the battle, right?), I have the best memories of swinging through our neighborhood drive-through and getting a bag of her favorites. We purchased the same thing every time—a ten-piece meal with a lemonade to drink. I'd help a bit with the fries and nuggets with loud protestation from the backseat. But there was only one problem: the total was the same for at least a year—$6.66.

Dressed in my clerical collar, I would sheepishly (goatishly?) hand over my credit card and chuckle every single time.

"This calls for wisdom: let anyone with understanding calculate the number of the beast, for it is the number for a person. Its number is six hundred sixty-six."[1] It is no surprise, with verses like this, that an interpreter from every generation arises who wants to calculate the end of the world. But the solution to this seemingly obscure math problem is quite simple. Most scholars today agree that 666 refers to a Hebrew transliteration of a villain that many of us can conjure even without much knowledge of Roman history—*Neron Kaisar*, Nero Caesar, or Nero Lord. In this simple math problem, Revelation takes a shot across the bow at the power of Rome, the threat of the beast, and the impending destruction of the empire at the center of the world. But before that happens, we must meet the enemy, its beasts, and the city at the center of everything.

My eldest daughter and I have been reading together since she couldn't read. She now reads in Spanish far better than I can. She could read any novel I put in front of her, and yet she tolerates my ongoing desire to read aloud to her because I have the best voices. One of our favorites has been the Harry Potter series. As of the writing of this book, we have not gotten to the great reveal (which I will now spoil right here for you), so she is clear that Professor Snape is a bad guy who always makes Harry's life worse. The book series lays out clear lines between good and evil, yet it gets a bit messier as the characters develop throughout the story. The beloved headmaster using people only to his eccentric ends, the young boy protecting his friends at all costs, and the ones we once thought were villains turning out to be the most selfless expression of love in the book. I fall into these stories because they show the complexity of humanity when it comes to good and evil. There is evil in the world. I will not deny it. When I look at the manifesto of the killer in Charleston, I see unvarnished evil. But our world is more often shaded with gray. Who gets to define what is evil and not? Powerful nations and powerful

---

1 Revelation 13:18

people often define evil in those who have less power, influence, or wealth. History is written through the vantage of the victor, shading the loser, regardless of their motivations, with the weight of loss. But perspective shifts when a different side of the story unveils our assumptions of good and evil, wrong or right, victor or loser.

Revelation is crystal clear on who is the villain and who are the heroes. Rome is the villain. The martyrs and the faithful are the heroes. There is no twist at the end, where Satan changes his mind and is turned toward the good. There is no character development of the beasts, where they rend their swords into plowshares and their spears into pruning hooks. Revelation puts the power of Rome, the emperor Nero, and the forces that fight on its behalf as simple servants of Satan, shallow characters bent on destruction and oppression, like zombies of the apocalypse. But who is this Satan? As with our understanding of hell, we will spend some time interrogating the cultural inheritance of images for the Prince of Darkness and learning how Scripture speaks of Satan. Like our conceptions of hell, our concepts of Satan have disastrous consequences as well. Two examples offer warnings of whether we ought to say another human is acting in alignment with Satan.

In 1980, a Canadian psychologist published a book entitled *Michelle Remembers* that told the story of one of his patients who had recovered repressed memories of abuse that had been perpetrated on her by a satanic cult. As reported by the *New York Times*, "Although its lurid claims were quickly challenged, the book was a best seller. Suddenly, it seemed, terror could be lurking in any neighborhood."[2] Three years later, in Manhattan Beach, California, accusations emerged of a childcare center that had been abusing children in tunnels dug under the grounds for satanic rites. In one of the most expensive trials of American history, the case became a national spectacle with "a variety of fantastical claims from interviews, including a 'goatman,' bloody animal sacrifices, a school employee who could fly and acts of violence

---

2 Alan Yuhas, "*It's Time to Revisit the Satanic Panic*," New York Times, *March 31, 2021.*

that left no physical trace."[3] Like the Salem witch trials, the witch hunts several centuries earlier, and the McCarthy trials, the so-called Satanic Panic was a time of shared moral concern, a moral panic that put all of society's anxieties onto an easy and terribly misplaced scapegoat—childcare centers and people working with children. Believing that satanic ritual was to blame for all of society's ills ignited hatred and distrust, tearing apart the fabric of local communities. How we think about Satan matters. The same moral panic over unsubstantiated abuse of children can be found in the ways that Q-Anon peddles in conspiracy theories about satanic worship by Democratic Party operatives in an organized cabal of pedophiles.[4] How we talk about Satan matters. Will we fan flames of moral panic, or will we confront the systems of evil that perpetuate wide-ranging destruction of the earth, our humanity, and the fabric of our communities?

Like I've mentioned before, we didn't have cable growing up. I promise it doesn't come up in therapy anymore. When I was home sick from school, I would try to watch some of the daytime TV shows. My favorite was *The Price Is Right*. Bob Barker carried that elegant little microphone, calling participants to "Come on down!" to try their hand at the coupon cutters' dream show with the promise of winning blenders and gas grills, jet skis and motorhomes, and finally, my favorite, a *new car*! But I always remember the show that was on at the same time—*The 700 Club*. I'll confess, it wasn't my favorite—A group of old dudes talking about the Bible, praying for the country, and getting pretty preachy on the talk show. It's probably for the best that I can't remember the content of any of the episodes I'm certain I watched. Its inflammatory host, Pat Robertson, was one of the foremost leaders in connecting conservative Evangelical Christians to the larger political movement of the GOP. Robertson frequently taught that homosexuality was a pathology that needed to be treated and,

---

3 Yuhas.

4 Noah Caldwell, Ari Shapiro, Patrick Jarenwattananon, and Mia Venkat, "America's Satanic Panic Returns—This Time Through QAnon," *National Public Radio*, May 18, 2021.

on *The 700 Club*, likened the offensive lives of gay people to Adolf Hitler and satanism. He decried women in leadership as feminists and denounced their ideology as "a socialist, anti-family political movement that encourages women to leave their husbands, kill their children, practice witchcraft, destroy capitalism and become lesbians." After the tragic earthquake in Haiti in 2010, Robertson went even further, purporting an incredibly racist revision of history by describing the Haitian people as a country that made a pact with the devil. Under Robertson's demonic interpretation, the Haitian people were facing the consequences of this pact in this heart-wrenching disaster that killed hundreds of thousands of people, destroyed much of the country's infrastructure, and wreaked havoc on its economy for a generation and beyond.[5] How we talk about Satan matters. How we envision evil in our world influences our politics, the way we speak to our neighbor, and how we might live in this world together. While I highlight Pat Robertson's horrendous quotes, vilifying the opposite political spectrum is not only a trait of the right side of the aisle. In this time of political division, we must be careful of discourse that aligns those who think differently than us with evil. It risks dehumanizing people who have real fears and hopes and dreams. And it sidesteps Revelation's insistence that victory is found in following the peaceful revolution of the Lamb who was slain.

A BRIEF HISTORY OF SATAN

Revelation provides one of the most significant developments of Satan in the Bible.[6] But the concept of Satan stretches back to the

---

5 Tori Otten, "A Compendium of Statements That St. Peter Might Be Asking Pat Robertson to Explain," *The New Republic*, June 8, 2023.

6 I provide a brief history of Satan in the paragraphs that follow. But for a more extensive look, I encourage you to read two books, Miguel De La Torre and Alberto Hernandez's *The Quest for the Historical Satan* (Minneapolis: Fortress Press, 2011) and Richard Beck's *Reviving Old Scratch: Demons and the Devil for Doubters and the Disenchanted* (Minneapolis: Fortress Press, 2016).

Hebrew Scriptures and blossoms in the time between the testaments. In pure translation of language, Satan is actually a Hebrew word, as opposed to the Greek word *diabolos* for the devil. Jesus is tempted by the devil in the wilderness, casts out demons into the unclean pigs, but reserves the title Satan for his closest follower when Peter questions the necessity of his death and resurrection: "Get behind me, Satan! You are a hindrance to me, for you are setting your mind not on divine things but on human things."[7]

Satan in the Hebrew Bible

We've already discussed in Chapter Three that the serpent present in the Garden of Eden is not the same character as Satan. While many interpreters across the centuries have drawn this connection (including Revelation), Genesis does not envision a powerful force of evil that convinces Adam and Eve to eat the fruit at the center of the garden. In the Hebrew Scriptures, Satan is actually never a proper noun. It doesn't refer to a name or a specific character. It is always connected with a definite article, which my English major tells me is the word *the*. In Hebrew, it is *ha* (the) *satan* (accuser). It is used only eighteen times in the Hebrew Scriptures, fourteen of those in the book of Job, an ancient parable where the satan drives a bargain with God for the fate of a beloved child of the divine.

Job is a vexing story that explores some of the cursed questions of humanity. Why do bad things happen to good people? Does God allow our suffering? Does God cause our suffering? Is God powerful enough to prevent or stop our suffering? It is the kind of book that often leaves readers with more questions than answers. The opening scene is no exception as we meet Job, who is described as a righteous man. *Ha satan*, the accuser, believes Job will curse God

---

7 Matthew 16:23

if the satan is allowed to take away the blessings that God has so graciously given him:

> One day the heavenly beings came to present themselves before the Lord, and Satan also came among them. The Lord said to Satan, "Where have you come from?" Satan answered the Lord, "From going to and fro on the earth, and from walking up and down on it." The Lord said to Satan, "Have you considered my servant Job? There is no one like him on the earth, a blameless and upright man who fears God and turns away from evil." Then Satan answered the Lord, "Does Job fear God for nothing? Have you not put a fence around him and his house and all that he has, on every side? You have blessed the work of his hands, and his possessions have increased in the land. But stretch out your hand now, and touch all that he has, and he will curse you to your face.[8]

If you read this passage looking for a being who has been evil from the beginning of time, it raises some very strange questions about God. Why would God strike a bargain with this evil being? Why would God tolerate the presence of evil alongside all the other heavenly beings? Is the evil being somehow equal to God?

If we skim by the mention of Satan in these verses, contemporary readers likely fill in the pictures conjured in our brain with pop-culture images of a fiery red character with horns and a pitchfork. It takes quite a bit of gymnastics to find an evil force in the Hebrew Scriptures like the caricature of Satan that we may have in our mind. When you hear the word Satan, images shaped by culture, popular and otherwise, likely come to your mind. They may involve the occult, or rituals that lead into scary places. They may involve angels and demons wrestling on either side of your shoulder, one side of your conscience leading toward virtue and the

---

8 Job 1:6-11

other toward vice. Perhaps you've heard that Satan is a fallen angel, who was cast out of heaven because he longed to be as powerful as God? This image is drawn largely from John Milton's *Paradise Lost*:

> O sun, to tell thee how I hate thy beams,
> That bring to my remembrance from what state I fell;
> how glorious once above thy sphere;
> Till pride and worse ambition threw me down,
> Warring in heaven against heaven's matchless King.[9]

Or maybe you've heard the description of Satan as Lucifer, the light-bringer? Dante's *Inferno*, which largely formalized the Italian language, introduces Lucifer in the final circle of hell, who has three heads that consume three traitors in eternity—Brutus, Cassius, and Judas. But the name Lucifer appears as a translation of the Greek word *phosphoros* (from which we get words like *phosphorescent*) referring to the morning star, or the planet Venus. Drawn from the prophet Isaiah, this image refers to the fall of the king of Babylon: "When the Lord has given you rest from your pain and turmoil and the hard service with which you were made to serve, you will take up this taunt against the king of Babylon . . . How you are fallen from heaven, *O Morning Star*, son of Dawn! How you are cut down to the ground, you who laid the nations low!"[10] What contemporary Bibles (like the NRSVue quoted here) translate as "morning star," the King James Version translates as Lucifer. The Hebrew word *hillel* definitely does not refer to the name of a heavenly being but is more likely a reference to the morning star that rises just before dawn.

Understood as *the accuser* (which is how the updated NRSVue translates *ha satan*), we can begin to watch the scene unfold like a courtroom drama where the righteousness of this man, Job, is called into question. The accuser offers God a few arguments, that Job has everything he would ever need and God has fenced him in

---

9 John Milton, *Paradise Lost*, Book IV, lines 37–41.
10 Isaiah 14:4, 12

with protection. Of course Job would praise God and act righteously. It is almost as if the satan is in the chair of a prosecutor, making a case against this man, Job. The satan is a prosecuting attorney, given enough leeway, without objection from the judge, God who presides over the trial. The book still asks many other cursed questions, but we can at least be alleviated of the satanic verses.

Satan in Between the Testaments

I bought my first true study Bible in college. I tried to skimp a little bit on the book lists at times, finding what I could in the library, sometimes getting last year's edition of a textbook so I could save more on a used copy. But the Bible I didn't want to come by cheaply. The Bible on the course list for Religion 100 was a hard-cover Oxford Annotated Bible with the Apocrypha. It is in fairly rough shape now, having been carried around campus in my messy backpack, written in with pencil, highlighted, and studied. The word *apocrypha* confused me from the beginning. I knew the Bible well going into college. I had lots of Scripture memorized. I knew where to find various characters and knew how to find verses quickly even if I couldn't remember the citation. I had never heard of the Apocrypha, so I opened those pages immediately to find out what was in it! The Table of Contents revealed titles I had never heard before—Bel and the Dragon, Tobit, Baruch, Esdras, Sirach, and Maccabees. Martin Luther did not advocate for removing these books from the Bible. In Luther's Bible, there are three main sections titled Old Testament, Apocrypha, and New Testament. My Oxford Bible follows the same scheme, along with the King James Version. My heart skipped beats reading its pages. Warnings from my memory sheet in parochial school swirled in my head: "Not many of you should become teachers, my brothers and sisters, for you know that we who teach will face stricter judgment."[11] And even from Revelation: "I warn everyone

---

11 James 3:1

who hears the words of the prophecy of this book: if anyone adds to them, God will add to that person the plagues described in this book; if anyone takes away from the words of the book of this prophecy, God will take away that person's share in the tree of life and in the holy city, which are described in this book."[12] Was I adding to the Scriptures by reading they? Were they to be trusted? Why had someone removed them from the leather-bound New International Version (NIV) that I received when I was baptized? Would I be judged more harshly by trusting these?

Religion classes added other hidden books that didn't even make the cut of Luther's Bible. We read entire gospels that I had never heard of, like the Gospel of Thomas, and encountered apocalyptic texts like Enoch and Jubilees. We discussed the Dead Sea Scrolls and how their discovery in Qumran resulted in a huge hubbub in scholarly circles. But why had no-one in church talked about these books? Why had I never encountered any of the conversation around more words about Jesus? Would they help me understand Jesus better, or would they lead me astray? For any who have grown up in various fundamentalisms, questions like this can be incredibly troubling. The word *apocrypha* literally means *hidden*, which certainly doesn't help, suggesting that the books were tucked away for the greater good. Whether in Luther's apocrypha (like Maccabees and Esdras) or extrabiblical or noncanonical (the Books of Enoch and the Book of Jubilees), the texts have nothing to fear. Some of them are strange and apocalyptic, like Enoch and Jubilees. Others, like Maccabees, tell historical stories important to Jewish traditions like Hannukah. I refer to them occasionally when I'm teaching Scripture now, to familiarize people with these books. But I also advise a bit of caution. There is wisdom in the tradition and canon shaped by our spiritual ancestors. The extrabiblical books were not in circulation for specific reasons in the story of Christianity. The Gnostic gospels like the Gospel of Thomas may have been excluded from the New Testament because they were written later. They may be

---

12 Revelation 22:18–19

rejected because they tell the story of Jesus from a vantage point that lost the argument in various ecumenical councils throughout history. The texts may not have been in circulation or shared in the same ways as the other canonical gospels. Or these texts may be out of the canon for reasons that have been lost to history. Likewise, the nonbiblical texts that we will examine about Satan are nonbiblical for reasons that are debated by scholars. We can learn from them, but they aren't the center of the scriptural witness. I share bits about them here because they help connect the Jewish understanding of Satan as a celestial prosecutor into a more malevolent vision of Satan as a being or force that opposes God's goodness in creation.

The Jewish people came into contact with a variety of religious expressions that had an impact on everything from the prophetic texts in the Hebrew Bible to the composition of the Torah. This is equally true of the New Testament. Revelation wrestles with how Christians ought to interact with other religious traditions in the Roman Empire and Paul writes letters to communities concerned about the influence of local religious and cultural practices. Some of us may hear this as a call to cling to some form of pure religion, but the story of Christianity, tracing all the way back to the earliest Hebrew Scriptures, adapts, changes, grows, and innovates alongside and in conversation with other religious traditions. The time in between the testaments was a particularly innovative season.

After living in exile in Babylon (which we'll talk about in just a few pages), the Jewish people came into contact with the Persians. The arrival of this new empire is celebrated in some of the later texts of the Old Testament, and Cyrus, their king, is described as a messianic figure, conquering Babylon and freeing the Jewish people in exile to return to their homeland. Isaiah sees Cyrus's mission as coming directly from the God of Israel: "I have aroused Cyrus in righteousness, and I will make all his paths straight; he shall build my city and set my exiles free, not for price or reward, says the Lord of hosts."[13] The Persians also brought their religious traditions and

---

13 Isaiah 45:13

beliefs with them, namely Zoroastrianism. Still a living religion today, Zoroastrianism has a strong vision of good and evil, where human beings and their moral choices are placed on a cosmic stage of spiritual battle between those forces. Many of us may know Zoroastrians from the magi who visit the baby Jesus in Matthew's Gospel. Even though our songs call them kings, these mages or astrologers were likely Zoroastrians who came to worship the child and offer gifts of gold, frankincense, and myrrh. Both Christianity and Judaism are shaped by their interaction with the strong dualism of Zoroastrianism, where the battleground between forces of good and evil is the human body. As they start to develop ideas of evil that oppose God's good work in the world, the spiritual battle also begins to mirror Zoroastrian claims that human salvation is a result of the spiritual battle between good and evil.

In these hidden, apocryphal texts written between the two testaments, stories of the Hebrew Bible are retold with a more robust vision of demons and devils who oppose God's good work. Books like First Enoch (a nonbiblical book written in this period) reinterpret strange texts in Genesis, perhaps drawing from traditions present in the composition of Genesis, to illustrate angels having sexual contact with humans, and to reveal the judgment of being cast out of heaven as fallen angels who teach humans sorcery and other forbidden practices. Another move in translation is that the Septuagint, or Greek translation of the Hebrew Bible, chose the word *daimon* to translate wooden idols, and the word *diabolos* is used to translate *ha satan*. As we've already discussed, translation brings with it a weight of cultural understanding. The Greek translation of the satan as a courtroom prosecutor eventually leads to the later Christian understanding of a "specific superhuman being who was the main adversary of God."[14]

Persian mages, ancient dualisms, and Greek translations may not feel as intimidating as they did in the beginning of our time together,

---

14 Miguel De La Torre and Alberto Hernandez, *The Quest for the Historical Satan* (Minneapolis: Fortress Press, 2011), 73.

but this is certainly the deep end of the theological swimming pool. All this is to say, people assume that many of our contemporary concepts come from the Bible. But this is simply not true. These extrabiblical texts and neighboring religious practices weave their way into our imagination as much as Dante's seven circles of hell or Milton's fallen angel.

Satan in the New Testament

Martin Scorsese has been a favorite filmmaker of mine. Always fascinated with religious themes, he obsessed for decades over the story of a missionary in feudal Japan, finally premiering *Silence* in 2013. In conversation with Pope Francis, Scorsese revealed that he is working on a new film about Jesus in 2023. But one of his early films retold Nikos Kazantzakis's classic novella *The Last Temptation of Christ*. A scrawny Willem Defoe plays Jesus in a clear departure from the countless retellings of the gospel narrative. The film was met with controversy among many Christians because it focused on the humanity of Jesus, including his temptation. Allegations of blasphemy aside (which miss the point of the film entirely), one of my favorite scenes shows Jesus being tempted in the wilderness, a story told in all three synoptic gospels (Matthew, Mark, and Luke). Defoe draws a circle in the desert, sitting on the rocks more like a modern mystic than an ancient rabbi, asking to hear God's voice clearly. He is visited by a snake who offers him a woman and family, a lion who tempts him with power over Rome itself, and a flame who offers the power of God over life and death. Jesus calls the name Satan, and the flame finally vanishes. Fascinating philosophers and religious alike, this scene also helps us understand the development of Satan in the New Testament.

In all three gospel accounts, Jesus is tempted in the wilderness for forty days, recalling the forty years that Moses leads the Israelites through the wilderness in Exodus. Mark offers only two verses, mentioning a temptation from Satan but providing little detail. Oddly enough, Mark includes the definite article in the Hebrew tradition, referring to *the* satan, but I have yet to find an

English translation that includes the proper article here, instantly personifying Satan into a proper name and, in essence, a super-being opposing God. Luke and Matthew refer consistently to the *diabolos*, the devil, covering roughly the same exchange between the devil and Jesus. Similar in repetition but not theme to Scorsese's scene, Jesus refuses three separate temptations from the devil: bread, power, and salvation. Jesus quotes Scripture and rebukes the devil, but only in Matthew's account does he use the word *Satan*, this time without the definite article, *the*. The New Testament uses the word *Satan* some thirty-six times and *diabolos* another thirty-seven times. The themes are certainly present across the gospels, epistles, Acts, and Revelation, but they are by no means an overwhelming thread in the narrative. In their *Quest for the Historical Satan* (which provides the groundwork for all of my brief history here), Miguel De La Torre and Alberto Hernandez see that the New Testament draws from existing (though nonbiblical) sources like Enoch to begin "the Christian practice of dividing the supernatural world into two opposing forces: the one true God along with God's angels versus Satan and his hordes of demons and fallen angels."[15]

Even though many of our ideas of Satan do not come from the Scriptures, it doesn't mean that these forces aren't real. One of my favorite acts as a pastor is to baptize children, usually infants, in our congregational worship services. At the beginning of the baptismal liturgy in our Lutheran tradition, we ask a threefold question that parallels Jesus's temptation in the wilderness. I look to the parents, smiling eagerly into the eyes of their children, grandparents witnessing with phone cameras poised for the big moment. Turning to the congregation, I ask the entire assembly to "profess your faith in Christ Jesus, reject sin, and confess the faith of the church." We continue with three questions that feel oddly otherworldly for a celebration of little babes in white dresses: "Do you renounce the devil and all the forces that defy God? Do you renounce the powers of this world

---

15 De La Torre and Hernandez, 74.

that rebel against God? Do you renounce the ways of sin that draw
you from God?"[16] In moments of holy wonder alongside children,
we pause to acknowledge that this world is incredibly broken, and
that there are forces that draw us from God, rebel against God, and
defy God. In a word, we acknowledge evil, our complicity in it, and
its hold on the world we live in.[17] Revelation is clear about the source
of evil in the ancient world and invites us to see analogues of that
evil empire in our own lives.

SATAN LIVES IN ROME

Revelation is perhaps the peak of Satan's development in the New
Testament, where we see a cosmic battle unfold in its apocalyptic
description. When Satan enters the scene, it is as a dragon, attempting
to devour Jesus, who has been born to the woman clothed in the stars.
But the dragon introduces two more beasts, who rise from the sea
and from the land, representing the economic and military power of
Rome. We have already discussed the calculation of the beast, Nero
Lord, which stands in stark contrast to one of the earliest Christian
confessions: Jesus is Lord. These two beasts arising from the dragon
are each a perversion of the lamb, who represents Jesus. Because of
their opposition to Christ, they have often been described in history
as anti-Christ. But there is no mention of a person called the (or an)
Anti-Christ in Revelation. It draws from a passage in 2 Thessalonians, describing "a lawless one," who is "destined to destruction"
and who "opposes and exalts himself above every so-called god or

---

16 *Evangelical Lutheran Worship* (Minneapolis: Augsburg Fortress,
2006), 229.

17 Richard Beck's book *Reviving Old Scratch: Demons and the Devil for
Doubters and the Disenchanted* (Minneapolis: Fortress Press, 2016) reclaims the
language of Satan and the devil as a means of resisting the many powers that
plague our world. His language cuts through the abusive spiritual warfare
that plagues the Evangelical world for a more exacting definition of the powers
that rebel against God. I find his argument exceedingly helpful in the secular
age that we find ourselves living in.

object of worship."[18] Rapture theology weaves various passages like this together into a unified narrative that the Bible as a whole simply does not support. And, again, the descriptions of the beasts within their own context give us much more interesting material to work with than speculating on who in recent memory or yet to come might be the anti-Christ.

The first beast emerges from the sea, where much of the economic might of the empire was carried, throughout the Mediterranean Sea. Other monsters were known to dwell in the sea throughout Scripture, such as Leviathan, which is the source of one of my favorite pieces of Scripture: "There the ships go to and fro, and Leviathan, which you formed to frolic there."[19] But Revelation's beast does not play on the beach. Its power and authority come from the dragon, the Satan (Revelation 13:2). It looks grotesquely like the lamb with "ten horns and seven heads, and on its horns were ten diadems, and on its heads were blasphemous names."[20] Even the evidence of Jesus's death is marked on the beast: "One of its heads seemed to have received a death blow, but its fatal wound had been healed."[21] We've already discussed how Nero is the embodiment of the beast, the servant of the Satan who wages destruction on the earth: "When the finishing touches were put onto the image of the beast, Nero sat for the portrait."[22]

Nero, who was dead when John wrote Revelation, was a villainous character of his own historical right. Nero had his wife executed, had his mother murdered, and was blamed by some for the great fire of Rome that burned for over seven days. Historians have noted that Nero held Christians responsible for the fires and burned many alive as punishment. But perhaps his most offensive campaign was sending an army to quell a Jewish uprising in Jerusalem in the year

---

18 2 Thessalonians 2:3-4
19 Psalm 104:26, NIV
20 Revelation 13:1
21 Revelation 13:3
22 Koester, 128

66 CE. After Nero's death by suicide, the war resulted in the siege of Jerusalem in 70 CE and the destruction of the temple. Nero was the face of this conquest, the villain behind the economic occupation of Rome, the leader behind the battalion that destroyed and desecrated the temple, the power that threatened to emerge, rise again, or even resurrect, further perverting the Christian gospel.

The beast's words echo the great offense of the temple's destruction: "It opened its mouth to speak blasphemies against God, blaspheming his name and his dwelling, that is, those who dwell in heaven."[23] Again, the temple was the dwelling of God, where people could trust God to always be. For the Jewish people who to this day hold the name of God as holy, set apart, not to even be uttered, blaspheming God's name is the worst offense. The common utterance of "Hail Caesar!" may have been heard from the streets while people traded coins with "Nero is LORD" written on them, completely defying a central prayer of Jewish spirituality to this day, the *Shema*: "Hear O Israel: The LORD our God is one LORD." Even today, our Jewish siblings do not utter, whisper, pronounce, or read the name of God written in four Hebrew letters. Any time you see the word LORD in your Bible with little uppercase letters, it is a stand-in for this name, which is so holy that it is not uttered, out of respect for the divine. Various Jewish traditions replace this word with *adonai* or *ha shem*, "Holy One" or "The Name," or more traditionally, "The LORD."

In one of the stranger resonances with Christian theology, a rumor emerged that Nero was still alive and that he would return with vengeance. It was a rumor that Christians may have heard alongside their own claims that Jesus was the lamb who was slain. The Apostle Paul strikes to the core of Christian teaching in his first letter to the Corinthians: "if Christ has not been raised, then our proclamation is in vain and your faith is in vain."[24] The first beast is a horrible caricature of the deepest mystery of Christian faith,

---

23 Revelation 13:6
24 1 Corinthians 15:14

for "we proclaim Christ crucified, a stumbling block to Jews and foolishness to gentiles."[25] Rome was already the occupying power in politics, where citizens held sway over ordinary folks. It dominated the marketplace through trade and monetary policy. And its military was a threat to any uprising. With the rumor of Nero's resurrection, Rome also entered the religious sphere by desecrating the mystery of Christian faith proclaimed in the earliest manuals of Christian worship: "Christ has died. Christ is risen. Christ will come again." The world worships the dragon because of the signs that this beast shows, but they ask rhetorical questions that early Christians would have heard loud and clear: "Who is like the beast, and who can fight against it?" Jesus is like the beast, but so unlike the beast. And the creator of the universe will fight against it for the sake of those who are being squashed by its domination.

John's contextual clues are so clear that he paints a picture of Rome as the dominating, cruel, oppressive force that it was. The beasts issue a religious, military, and economic challenge to the empire. John religiously incites the churches to rise against the subtle worship of the emperor, where the common phrase was Caesar is Lord (*Neron Kaisar*). Its military challenge is in the result of the final battle, where Rome's beasts do not conquer Jerusalem, but the Lamb is a victor of a different sort, bringing heaven to earth, ushering in a new Jerusalem, and bringing creation back to Eden, where the tree of life heals all the nations of the earth. Its economic challenge draws a line in the sand for participating in public banquets (an issue discussed throughout the New Testament), where free food was given to those who worshipped the cult of the emperor, literally the remnants of sacrifice offered to the servant of the satan. The emergence of the second beast makes the economic point even more clearly.

The second beast is another perversion of the vision of the Lamb: "it had two horns like a lamb, and it spoke like a dragon. It exercises all the authority of the first beast on its behalf, and it makes the earth and its inhabitants worship the first beast, whose fatal wound had

---

25 1 Corinthians 1:23

been healed."[26] Even further, it shows great signs (fire raining from heaven[27]) that convince even more people to follow the beast, asking them to make graven images of the beast, even animating some of those idols to speak for themselves.[28]

But the economics of the second beast further clarify analogy with Rome. The economic might of the empire may have been an even more influential tool of coercion than outright violence or military might. We finally hear of the mark of the beast, which is what I worried about in that Cold Stone lobby when folks walked in with ashes on their forehead. "Also, it causes all, both small and great, both rich and poor, both free and slave, to be given a brand on the right hand or the forehead, so that no one can buy or sell who does not have the brand, that is, the name of the beast or the number for its name."[29]

Contemporary rapture fearmongers liken the mark of the beast to a wide variety of economic tools. Bar codes, for example, are a strange symbol that seemingly connect everyone on the planet. It is impossible to purchase things without them. Social security numbers function as identity markers to gain access to credit and, in our increasingly cashless society, credit cards can track purchases of anyone on the planet. During the Covid-19 pandemic, as vaccines became more widely available, conspiracy theories and misinformation were everywhere on social media. But it was quite difficult for social media platforms to police religious content intertwined with vaccine skepticism and misinformation. Creators would share videos and memes linking the vaccine, government-issued vaccine cards, electronic medical records, and even masking to examples of the mark of the beast. As concert venues and restaurants in major metropolitan areas required proof of vaccination to enter, conspiracy theories like Q-Anon linked "coastal elites" to policing the pandemic. White Evangelicals remain one of the most vaccine-resistant

---

26 Revelation 13:11–12
27 Revelation 13:13
28 Revelation 13:14–15
29 Revelation 13:16–17

communities in the United States, perhaps largely due to the spread of misinformation that links life-saving vaccines to this mark of an ancient beast.[30] Revelation's vision for the mark of the beast, however, may be far simpler than QR codes, social security numbers, or vaccine cards.

Ancient coins bear the mark of the beast, an image of the emperor with their name and title, for example Neron Kaiser, Nero Caesar, or Nero Lord. Needing to handle coins in order to participate in the life of commerce, the necessity of using Roman money served as a constant reminder to the intertwined power of the cult of the emperor. Religion, economics, politics, power, and military might all served the beast of empire. Alongside the *shema* prayer and confession outlined in Deuteronomy is a command to "Bind [these words] as a sign on your hand, fix them as an emblem on your forehead."[31] The insistence to wear the mark of the beast on hand and forehead stands in stark contrast to the tradition of confessing devotion to God, whose love lit the stars. Each beast is like a political cartoon of the Roman Empire, emboldening the few who might resist, offering power through ridicule of the seemingly powerful giant. But if people weren't seeing the connection yet, a reference to a more ancient empire than Rome would make the case abundantly clear.

NAPS DISMANTLING PYRAMIDS

Resistance to the economic might of Rome may have seemed impossible to early Christian communities. The cult of the emperor was everywhere, vying for their attention and devotion in great public feasts, rituals in local temples, and the everyday practice of exchanging coins. But Revelation provides a method of resistance that goes

---

30 Elizabeth Dwoskin, "On social media, vaccine misinformation mixes with extreme faith" *Washington Post*, February 16, 2021, https://www.washingtonpost.com/technology/2021/02/16/covid-vaccine-misinformation-evangelical-mark-beast/

31 Deuteronomy 6:8

all the way back to the beginning. Just as the number seven occurs throughout the text, so too the seventh day of creation is a gift to the people of Israel as they escape the clutches of Pharaoh's economy of enslavement. When Moses recounts the gift of the Ten Commandments in Deuteronomy, the text draws the people into a shared memory: "But the seventh day is a Sabbath to the Lord your God . . . Remember that you were a slave in the land of Egypt, and the Lord your God brought you out from there with a mighty hand and an outstretched arm; therefore the Lord your God commanded you to keep the Sabbath day."[32] The Exodus narrative echoes throughout Revelation. Sets of seven tragedies appear in a constant drumbeat from chapter six all the way through chapter sixteen. Seven seals need to be opened in order to read the scroll. Seven trumpets send fire and brimstone from above, poison the fresh drinking water, locusts that sting like scorpions, and millions of battle horses. Seven bowls of God's wrath are poured out as seven plagues for the earth below. If the final reference to seven plagues isn't a clear enough reference to the plagues that God brings on Egypt, the heavenly assembly "sing the song of Moses, the servant of God, and the song of the Lamb."[33]

Readers are dizzied by verse after verse of terrible things happening on earth. It reminds me of one of my favorite YouTube comedians, Julia Nolke. In the midst of the pandemic, she released a series of videos in which she visits her past self to explain what has just happened in the months before. Remembering the year 2020 probably brings chills to all of our spines, just as Julia's earlier self is completely dumbfounded by the events that happen just around the corner in time. It is easy to become disoriented in this section of Revelation, reading passages that confront some of the notions we have about God's love. These terrible visions open questions about whether God *causes* all the pain on the earth below. Why would a loving God cause so much pain? But the Exodus narrative, once again, can provide

---

32 Deuteronomy 5:14–15
33 Revelation 15:2

us a way to see how God works in and through the bowls of wrath, plagues of locusts, and the terror that takes place on the earth.

In the Exodus narrative, Pharaoh does not want to let the Hebrew people go. Moses goes to him time after time, asking Pharaoh to let God's people go. Plague after plague (ten in Exodus) visit the nation of Egypt. The Nile River turns to blood. Frogs, lice, flies, and locusts devastate the crops and the people. Disease kills the livestock, boils cover everyone, hail wrecks the nation, and darkness blots out the sun. Pharaoh is resolute, never freeing the people. It is a rhythm in the storytelling. A plague occurs, and Pharaoh says, "no way." But the specific language of the hardening of Pharaoh's heart provides us with an entry point to the destruction in Revelation. In six of the plagues of Exodus, Pharaoh hardens his own heart, doubling down on the economy that Egypt built on the bodies of the Hebrew people. Inverted from the original blessing at the beginning of Genesis, where God calls creation good after each and every day, Pharaoh hardens his heart against the cries of the people for freedom. But in four of the plagues, God hardens Pharaoh's heart. Before the final plague, Moses speaks to Pharaoh in emotional terms, pleading Pharaoh to release the people: "Then there will be a loud cry throughout the whole land of Egypt, such as has never been or will ever be again."[34]

The final plague is challenging to read, as the same death is visited upon Egypt that they perpetuated against the sons of the Hebrew people at the beginning of the narrative, killing every firstborn son in the land. Moses tells the people of Israel to sacrifice a lamb and paint the blood above the doorpost of the houses so that death might pass over those houses. The cry echoes across Egypt, and all of the Egyptians send the Hebrew people packing, reversing the narrative and *begging* them to leave. They flee all the way to the Red Sea when Pharaoh has yet another change of mind, and "The Lord hardened the heart of Pharaoh king of Egypt, and he pursued the Israelites, who were going out boldly."[35] This final hardening of Pharaoh's heart

---

34 Exodus 11:6
35 Exodus 14:8

leads to the destruction of all his chariots and soldiers, drowned in the crashing waves of the Red Sea. Pharaoh's heart is hardened because of the pattern of abuse of the people. Consistently denying them humanity and freedom and dignity, Pharaoh will pursue occupation of them until it destroys everything he has built. This is the way of empire, the way of Rome, the way of Babylon, and the way that God undoes the powers of this planet. Justice will not be denied and there is no way for Pharaoh to avoid the consequences of his abuses. Empires fold in on themselves, fracturing due to their own inadequacies. For a people on the underside of the dominant historical, religious, economic, and military narrative, the vision that Revelation draws from the Exodus story is good news and gift.

Further, the Sabbath was a gift of resistance to the people of Israel. Over and against Pharaoh's endless economic oppression, the people were granted a day for rest, for time with God, for the presence of family and community. Linking the Sabbath practice to memory of slavery in Egypt provides us with another key to Revelation's invitation to embody resistance to empire. Every time we hear one of the challenging segments of plague or war or disaster or beast or Satan or lake of fire, John is drawn up into the heavenly worship service, where Sabbath is union with God. Sabbath is a gift of life-giving practice for a people whose humanity is stripped away. Sabbath is a practice of resistance against the economics of empire, then or now, that insist humans are only the sum of what they accomplish or build or make. Sabbath is an act of worshipping the creator, who ordained rest as an essential blessing for humanity and for all of creation.[36]

Seven upon seven upon seven reminding the ancients and readers today that we need the life-giving presence of God. I first heard of the revolutionary practice of taking naps from Professor Rollie Martinson, who napped every day, taking time underneath his desk

---

36 Sabbath is a powerful theme across Scripture. While I only hint at it in this section, you can find much more in a wonderful little book by Dr. Brueggemann. Walter Brueggemann, *Sabbath as Resistance: Saying No to a Culture of Now* (Nashville: Westminster John Knox Press, 2014).

for rest and rejuvenation. I've since become a great fan of napping. When our kids were little and my nights were often sleepless, I would take thirty minutes in the youth room of our church, which was quiet during the week. I'd lie on the couch and simply sleep for thirty or forty-five minutes. Rest is sacred work and isn't something we ought to take lightly. Our consumer economy too often turns the practice of rest into something else we need to consume—a massage membership or a swanky spa, wellness credits with insurance companies and subscriptions to exercise platforms. In other corners of our hustle culture, rest is something that will help us keep moving, that will make us more productive or better employees. Tech companies in the Silicon Valley are famous for offering wellness packages, amenities, and nap spaces for their employees, all under the hope that they'll spend yet more time on their campus and become more productive. But rest is not something that humans need to purchase or earn or work our way toward. Rest is gift, and rest is resistance. Tricia Hersey is the founder and creator of The Nap Ministry, an Instagram ministry that boasts nearly 600 thousand followers, and has written the *New York Times*-bestselling book *Rest Is Resistance: A Manifesto*. Called the Nap Bishop, Hersey rebukes the notion that rest makes us better employees or helps us produce more:

> Our drive and obsession to always be in a state of "productivity" leads us to the path of exhaustion, guilt, and shame. We falsely believe we are not doing enough and that we must always be guiding our lives toward more labor. The distinction that must be repeated as many times as necessary is this: We are not resting to be productive. We are resting simply because it is our divine right to do so.[37]

We may not be building pyramids today, but there is a growing frustration with grind culture, the ongoing demands of a consumer economy, the limitations of capitalism, and the inheritance of white

---

37 Tricia Hersey, *Rest Is Resistance: A Manifesto* (Little, Brown Spark, 2022).

supremacy in an American system built on enslaved Black bodies. Social media circles talk about "quiet quitting," sell devices to disguise mouse clicks from office surveillance programs, and share tips on how to set boundaries with your boss. Rest is about reclaiming our humanity, receiving a gift and a right from the creator who rested while creating all that exists. Revelation rests in the ongoing call of worship, moments drawn into God's presence, where rest is marked by the songs of the angels, a jubilant respite from the chaos unfolding on earth below. For the Nap Bishop, this is prophetic, imaginative work: "Yes, it's about literal naps, but it's also about imagination work, justice work. It's about education: We need to understand what the systems are doing to us, so that we can resist in a way that is fruitful for us."[38] Revelation fiercely opposes Pharaoh of old, Nero of present, and any emperor, empire, or empirical economy yet to come. Whether in the flesh of a person or the practices of a corporation or the systems and structures of an economy, the end of humanity is rest with God. And God continues to sustain creation through the gift of the sabbath—a gift for humanity that stretches from the beginning of time itself.

BABYLON TO BUST

Before we can make our way to the new Jerusalem, the beautiful city descending from heaven with its pearly gates flung wide open, we are introduced to another ancient city. Babylon was an ancient enemy of the Hebrew people. Babylon had conquered Jerusalem and deported masses away from their homeland, destroying the temple and wiping away the memory of their culture in the process. Prophetic texts across the Hebrew Bible recall this tragedy, asking cursed questions of what the people did to deserve such a calamity,

---

38 Tricia Hersey, quoted in, Melonyce McAfee, "The Nap Bishop Is Spreading the Good Word: Rest," *New York Times*, October 13, 2022, https://www.nytimes.com/2022/10/13/well/live/nap-ministry-bishop-tricia-hersey.html

whether God hears the cries or has turned the divine face away, and the haunting lament of "How long?"

The beasts of Rome, the dragon Satan, the emperor himself, Nero, have led people in their economy of oppression. But the final scene of judgment does not take place at the pearly gates, with Peter sorting sheep and goats. It is also not a great battle where Jesus slaughters the occupying army like the D-Day invasion at Normandy. Rather the final scene of consequence for the empire happens in a courtroom.

John describes Babylon as a "great whore who is seated on many waters, with whom the kings of the earth have engaged in sexual immorality and with the wine of whose prostitution the inhabitants of the earth have become drunk."[39] In stark contrast with the woman who gives birth to Jesus in chapter twelve, this harlot rides a scarlet beast in the wilderness "and on her forehead was written a name, a mystery: 'Babylon the great, mother of whores and of earth's abominations.'"[40] The image is a darkly comedic political cartoon, showing the wealth and opulence of Rome's "gold and jewels and pearls."[41] The angel offers even greater clarity of the meaning of this vision, just like the invitation to decode 666 by referring to Rome's common description of the city set on seven hills: "This calls for a mind that has wisdom: the seven heads are seven mountains on which the woman is seated."[42] The source of its power and intoxication for the nations of the earth is that it is "drunk with the blood of the saints and the blood of the witnesses to Jesus."[43]

This vision is incredibly dense and confusing and has led to subordination and oppression of women throughout the story of Christianity. As Barbara Rossing writes, "In the history of art and literature, the whore of Babylon has become the ultimate 'Jezebel' in most people's minds, personifying the 'fatal attraction' of the powerful evil temptress who seduces her victims with her irresistible golden cup

---

39 Revelation 17:1–2
40 Revelation 17:5–6
41 Revelation 17:4
42 Revelation 17:9
43 Revelation 17:6

of fornications. Read literally, this image can fuel the worst misogynist fantasies."[44] Fueling the fantasy of fanatics like Frollo in *The Hunchback of Notre Dame*, Evangelical insistence on purity culture today, ongoing "slut-shaming" of women and female sexual appetites across our culture, images like this in Revelation have also sparked witch trials and worldwide violence against women. But this "literal" reading of the text misses its clear reference to Babylon, Rome, and all of the empires that pillage the earth, human beings, and the abundance of God's creation. Rossing contends, "The charge of 'fornication' or 'trafficking' against Babylon/Rome has nothing to do with sex but is rather an economic charge—Rome lives by its predatory trade, trafficking in resources from the farthest points of the Roman Empire . . . What is highlighted throughout this entire scene is the economic and political critique of Rome, not a critique of women."[45]

Babylon and the nations of the earth turn on the whore, "they and the beast will hate the whore; they will make her desolate and naked; they will devour her flesh and burn her up with fire."[46] It was rumored in the ancient world that Nero was the cause of the great fire of Rome in 64 CE that burned much of the city across a week-long blaze. But the city does not receive judgment until the final courtroom scene, where victory is proclaimed over the horrors that Rome has perpetrated over the entire world. Angels sing from heaven indictments of Rome's crimes against humanity "for all the nations have fallen from the wine of the wrath of her prostitution."[47] The truth of Rome's violence and exploitation must be heard by the heavenly court and the faithful watching patiently for judgment. The court documents lay out the case against the rulers of the nations who "lived in luxury with her,"[48] the merchants who profited from the trade of the empire, and the shipmasters and seafarers, who chart the goods across the world. The courtroom drama confronts the religious, economic, and

---

44 Rossing, 132.
45 Rossing, 133.
46 Revelation 17:15
47 Revelation 18:3
48 Revelation 18:9

military might of the empire and introduces consequences that will end the oppression "for mighty is the Lord God who judges her."[49] As Rossing writes, "People who cry out for justice in the world, who are oppressed by tyrants, need to know that there is a divine law court or tribunal before which their case can be brought."[50]

In 1996, Nelson Mandela created the world's first Truth and Reconciliation Commission to be chaired by one of the greatest preachers, activists, and spiritual leaders of our time, Bishop Desmond Tutu. After generations of racist violence from the apartheid system in South Africa, this tribunal was tasked with telling the truth of this period in the nation's history, naming the ways that white South Africans were responsible for seven thousand political deaths and human rights violations of more than nineteen thousand people. The Truth and Reconciliation Commission utilized restorative justice practices that centered the stories of victims, inviting truth to be named and heard, while pursuing forgiveness and reconciliation rather than vengeance and retribution. Desmond Tutu wrote about the process in *No Future Without Forgiveness*, articulating the theological violence that apartheid had inflicted: "One of the most blasphemous consequences of injustice, especially racist injustice, is that it can make a child of God doubt that he or she is a child of God."[51] The truth and reconciliation process provided a vision for nations to confront the atrocities of the past and "affirm the dignity and personhood of those who for so long had been silenced, had been turned into anonymous, marginalized ones."[52] Projects have sprung up across the world to follow the lead of South Africa's process. In 2003, the Greensboro Truth & Reconciliation Commission became the first commission in North America with a mandate to "to examine the context, causes, sequence and consequence of the events of November 3, 1979 for the purpose of healing transformation for the

---

49 Revelation 18:8

50 Rossing, 131

51 Desmond Tutu, *No Future Without Forgiveness* (New York: Image Books, 2000).

52 Desmond Tutu, *No Future Without Forgiveness*.

community."[53] While the commission did not secure government sanction for its work, a private group of citizens led a process to tell the truth about the Greensboro massacre, where five people were killed in violence perpetuated by Ku Klux Klan and American Nazi Party members through complicit inaction by the Greensboro Police Department. Calls for national processes continue to gain momentum but have yet to materialize in response to structural racism and chattel slavery in the United States.[54] First Nations and Canadian government leaders led the Truth and Reconciliation Commission of Canada on a national scale from 2008 to 2015 to document the widespread and horrific abuse of boarding schools across Canada.

Whether local or large-scale, each of these commissions seeks to confront the truth and find a way forward. Revelation does not articulate a fully restorative vision for the end of Babylon, Rome, and the empires of the earth. Justice comes to these forces "for her sins are heaped high as heaven, and God has remembered her iniquities."[55] The consequences for Rome are not vengeance, however, or occupation from a more powerful force, or a violent battle over the beasts. Rather, Rome faces the result of its own consumption: "Render to her as she herself has rendered, and repay her double for her deeds; mix a double dose for her in the cup she mixed. As she glorified herself and lived luxuriously, so give her a like measure of torment and grief."[56] While Revelation may not follow the pathway of a truth and reconciliation commission, it articulates the same end goal—an end to the alluring power of empire that allows few to profit off the exploitation of the many. The trial in Revelation provides an avenue to name empire's continued hold on our own lives today, through unjust economic policies, social structures, systems of inequity, and

---

53 "Greensboro Truth & Reconciliation Commission," https://greensborotrc.org/

54 Sarah Souli, "Does America Need a Truth and Reconciliation Commission?" *Politico*, August 16, 2020, https://www.politico.com/news/magazine/2020/08/16/does-america-need-a-truth-and-reconciliation-commission-395332

55 Revelation 18:5

56 Revelation 18:6–7

political divisions. Remembering the ancient empire of Babylon as a stand-in for Rome calls forth the powers of empire that echo in contemporary religious, military, and economic injustice.

The beasts are eventually destroyed after the trial of Babylon, the great city that represents the destruction of the first temple and the Roman destruction of the second temple. Babylon is Rome, controlled by the Satan, the great deceiver. Through the beastly expressions of Rome's military, economic, and religious occupation and oppression, Revelation calls us to acknowledge the forces of empire that continue to plague our world. Babylon falls, and the beasts are destroyed, "thrown into the lake of fire that burns with sulfur."[57] The dragon's fate is similar, first bound by an angel who "threw him into the pit and locked and sealed it over him, so that he would deceive the nations no more, until the thousand years were ended. After that he must be let out for a little while."[58] These thousand years have critical importance to the rapture theologies we discussed earlier. They filter these (unbiblical and unhelpful) interpretations into pre- and post-millennial camps who argue where we live on the timeline of Satan's destruction and when Jesus will return on that timeline. Revelation cares not about linear time. It is cyclical, returning the action to worship and the final vision of God's goodness because the end is the beginning. After the destruction of the beasts and the dragon, Revelation concludes with the three visions we have been reading together throughout this book: new creation, new city, and new garden. God does not start over with a new world. God sustains the beauty of creation through the worst that an empire can throw at it. God contains the impact of evil, casts it into its own destruction, preserves the faithful, and promises goodness and healing for all nations. So, of course, we end where we began, with a beautiful vision of God's home among mortals, where the streets of the city sing the hymns of praise to God's presence among us all, and where the tree of life bears fruit for all to eat and leaves for the healing of all nations.

---

57 Revelation 19:20
58 Revelation 20:3

Conclusion

The End Is the Beginning

My eldest daughter lives with a rare auto-immune disorder that causes her white blood cells to attack her platelets, the particulates responsible for clotting, slowing, and eventually stopping bleeding. In the early moments of kindergarten, she received weekly blood draws to make sure that her body had enough platelets to do all of the normal kid activities like jumping off the diving board, sledding down a snowy hill, cartwheels on the grass, or jumping off the swings at recess. If her platelets were dangerously low, we would have to restrict some of her favorites. One of the side effects of her condition is that she bruises more easily than most kids. A bump on the knee can turn her skin purple and green and orange for weeks, resulting in more than one raised eyebrow at our parenting.

As I've described to you many of my Bible bruises and dogmatic dilemmas throughout the pages of this book, I've come to realize that my daughters will not have the same inheritance that I have had. Like many post-Evangelical parents, I take the faith formation of our kids very seriously. We talk about the Bible, about stories and questions that the girls have. We are open about our doubts, about the uncertain bits of Scripture, the corners of the story that curricula avoid, and the cursed questions that rattled my teachers growing up. Some of you may have read my stories of deconstruction with curiosity, having little reference point in your own story and memory. Others may have read these pages with a nodding head and the knowing glance of someone who has stories of your own to share. I hope that you find balm in your journey and promise in the pages of Scripture that were once used to bruise. Even though my eldest has frequently complained about my writing as "boring," I hope that some day it can provide an origin into a deepened faith. Anytime we are courageous enough to ask cursed questions, anytime we are bold enough to challenge the convictions of the room, anytime we are curious enough to splice open the threads of a story that is far more complex than a soundbite or a doctrinal statement, we find a new beginning for faith to develop, deepen, and evolve.

Revelation is a complicated book, made even more complicated by the centuries of misinterpretation that fill our minds as we open its pages. But I believe firmly that finding a way to read Revelation has helped me begin to heal the bruises that pain me and the people I love. I hope it might help you too. I've dropped little hints about the end of this tale as clues along the way, visions of the heartbeat of a promise that pulses through every page of the book at the end of the Bible. Using three of the most beautiful pictures in all of the Bible, Revelation draws the veil thinly between the here and the not-yet, beckoning all of us forward with the promise of a new creation, a new city, and a new garden.

As the page turns to the glorious visions found in Revelation 21–22, the first vision offers an invitation into God's new creation. Like the beginning verses of Scripture, when God speaks, something happens. God's voice is not a static doctrine or a stagnant dogma. God speaks with creativity, imagination, invitation, and affirmation. "See I am making all things new."[1] God is not a cosmic watchmaker who sets creation spinning and watches detached from afar. Instead, God wipes every tear from their eyes in one of the greatest images of intimacy in Scripture. When God speaks a final word over creation, it is a sort of benediction that also mirrors the blessing that God speaks in Genesis:

---

1 Revelation 21:5

"It is done! I am the Alpha and the Omega, the Beginning and the End. To the thirsty I will give water as a gift from the spring of the water of life. Those who conquer will inherit these things, and I will be their God, and they will be my children."[2] The completion of creation is actually a beginning in and of itself. God doesn't step away from this new paradise but leans closer, beckoning forth new life around every corner. Yes, God is the alpha and the omega, the first and last letters of the alphabet, but God has been there all along the way, with every letter, every verse, every jot and every tittle. God is sustaining everything that exists with the selfsame love that lit the stars.

The new city emerges next "coming down from heaven from God" in a marriage scene between the Lamb and the new Jerusalem, where "mourning and crying and pain will be no more." Clearly contrasted to the courtroom defeat of Babylon, Jesus's work takes shape in the midst of the city, the holy habitation of God's presence among human beings and all of creation. God is in the midst of the city; it shall not be moved. With no need for a temple, the city itself pulses with the heartbeat of the creator, dancing with love and life. This massive city stretches wide enough for all of the nations in the world to bring their glory and celebrate the end of empire and the coming of God's rule, where "God will be with them and they will be his peoples." The gates are not guarded by angels or rulers but are instead flung wide open to welcome the beautiful diversity that God has designed humanity to embody.

Finally, a new garden grows in the middle of the city, where the tree of life straddles a streaming river that flows from the throne of God and the Lamb. Rather than the sign of the beast or the name of Babylon, people walk through the garden with the name of the Lamb on their foreheads. In our baptism liturgy, we mark people with a symbol of the cross on their foreheads with the words, "You are marked with the cross of Christ forever." God claims each of us in the waters of baptism, in the waters of new creation, sustains our lives, and calls forth a new creation in each of us. Just like the new

---

2 Revelation 21:6–7

life we celebrate in baptism, Revelation marks the end of empire and the beginning of something else entirely, a new story for creation.

My hope is that Revelation might spark a beginning for you.

Where faith feels stale or stagnant,
    I hope these visions offer a spark of electric belonging.

Where doctrine and dogma chafe, itch, or bruise,
    I pray that this promise is balm for a weary soul.

When imagination is limited by the way
    we've always done things or
    the artificial constraints of a stagnant system,
        I hope these scenes rattle loose
            disruptive delights of potential.

Where churches get stuck preserving institutions
    instead of spilling forth good news,
        I pray the witness of the saints inspires visions of the elders
            and dreams of the youth.

Where gates slam shut to maintain order or conclusive identity,
    I pray the Spirit of the Living God will shake the hinges and
        fling open the doors
        to beckon the belonging that
        Jesus welcomes for all of God's creation.

When the forces of this world rage and rebel and rampage,
    I pray that
        the creator of the Stars of Night,
        the Pantocrator,
        the Sustainer of all that was and is and will forever be,
        the Lamb that rises with the morning,
        the Alpha and Omega and open ending of the story,
        the streets of the new city,
        the garden at the center of all that will be,
        the new beginning of us all

might wipe your tears, bind up your wounds,
   and sing the first words of welcome
   that begin your next chapter.

My daughters may not have the same ending to their story, the same fears in their bones. They may not be bruised by the Bible or deconstruct the same dogma. But I will make sure that they meet the God who is making all things new for each of them, for you, and for me.

Acknowledgments

While many mornings felt like a wrestling match with my keyboard, a Bible, and a stack of bookish friends, so many people helped make this possible. Thank you to Meta Herrick Carlson for making coffee with cinnamon (who knew?) and typing while I talked a proposal into existence. Thank you to Ellie Roscher for coaching me through moments of trepidation and procrastination, and for grounding me in adding to the word count. Lisa Kloskin, I can't believe you trusted a seminary classmate with a book deal. Thank you for believing in this project, cheering me on, holding my feet to the fire, and putting up with my delays. The book is bound and on shelves because of your careful edits, thoughtful collaboration, and endless encouragement. Thanks to Eric Barreto for reading the manuscript, catching my Bible mistakes, and helping shape the vision of this book. Your patience, grace, and encouragement mean the world to me. The entire team at Broadleaf Books who publicized, designed, copyedited, and marketed a first-time author, you have my eternal gratitude. Thank you to St. Andrew Lutheran Church for providing sabbatical time to write, dream, explore, and delight, tilling the soil of creativity. To my pastoral colleagues, especially Peter and Gail for believing in my ability to write this, even when it meant I was distracted and spluttering apocalyptic verses in staff meetings. To the Church Anew team (Tim, Mary, and many more) for constantly delighting in new things being brought into the world, for setting a broader table of welcome for those curious and confused about the corners of Scripture. To Natalia and Emmy, hosts of Cafeteria Christian, and to all the Cafeterians who create community for people whose Bible bruises match my own. For the leaders who surrounded me with support in retreats and Zoom calls through Leadership on the Way—Dan, Sarah, Kara, and Josh, you keep me going! For a truly mystical session of Artist's Way led by Danielle Shroyer that got me through the worst block of creativity—Natalia, Jenny, John, Carrie, Adam, Charlie, Meta, Nathan, Eric—you remind me that the magic is always in the air. For Hannah—you picked up so much of my slack when I was in the throes of getting words on the page. I cannot thank you enough for creating space for this project to come to be. For A, you wrote your own books in scraps of paper with staples and crayons, tossing shade on my boring book. Keep on writing and creating and playing and dreaming. For DK, may your smile and laugh echo in endless praise like the angels' chorus. For all the churches that raised me, for my family, my grandparents and parents, and all who have helped form a faith that just keeps evolving, thank you for your patience and pride. For you, dear reader, I hope this book helps excavate any fear of the end so that you might dance in a garden, delight in a city, and sing endless praise for a God of new beginnings and endless possibilities.